A Gift for

_____

From

_____

Date

_____

"Educators have one of the hardest roles in society. Huesmann meets readers where they are with biblically sound reminders that God is with teachers in the midst of their day. With this book on your desk you're sure to feel every day is a good day to be a teacher."

—**Tez Brooks**, former Communications Leader for Intl. School Project and author of YouVersion's Hope for School Teachers

"Teaching children is a demanding profession. Most teachers would benefit from regular encouragement and inspiration. This devotional addresses the real-life situations and feelings of teachers and delivers inspiration and hope. This book is a delightful gift for any teacher you want to encourage."

—**James C. Galvin**, EdD, Cocreator and Co-Senior Editor of The Life Application Study Bible

"Now more than ever, educators are searching for meaningful resources to kindle joy in their work. Gretchen's devotions unpack and apply biblical truths, offering refreshing encouragement that is desperately needed by educators across all age groups and settings. Each entry reminds readers that God's grace, purpose, and strength are what fuels them and their ministries to students."

—**Tosca Grimm, EdD**, Program Chair at Concordia University Department of Graduate Education; Preschool Director of Amazing Grace Christian Preschool in Pensacola

"Gretchen Huesmann's extensive classroom experience is clearly evident in these practical yet insightful devotions for teachers. With prayers included, these short, powerful devotions will be sure to equip, empower, and bless anyone teaching God's children."

—**Steven Buuck, EdD**, CEO of Faith Lutheran Middle School and High School, Las Vegas

"With heartfelt compassion, Gretchen offers some much-needed balm to the wounded teacher. Her personal teaching journey and vibrant confidence in Jesus, coupled with the real-life vignettes in each devotion, give us access to the challenges and hope experienced by teachers today. The reality that "teaching has changed so much in recent years" is met with promise and resolve."

—**Pastor Jeff Meyer**, author of *Fear Not, Dream Big, & Execute* and *The Dream Primer*

"As a career educator, Gretchen Huesmann knows the trials and discouragements that teachers face on a daily basis. But Gretchen also knows the joys and the source of her strength. Her devotions speak to the heart of teachers who strive to impart knowledge and sound life principles into their students, even when they or their parents don't appreciate their efforts. Every educator should have a copy of this well-written, concise, and applicable devotional book to turn to when they're stressed and in need of encouragement."

—**Marilyn Turk**, author of *The Escape Game*

"Gretchen takes real-life examples of life in the classroom and beautifully ties them into learning from scripture. Through her own experience, she recognizes the many challenges of being a teacher and turns them into opportunities and encouragement to keep Jesus first and foremost in every day and to be more deeply invested in the lives of students, parents, and colleagues."

—**Debbie Arfsten**, EdD, Program Chair of Director of Christian Education, Concordia University

"This devotional is just what I needed, providing encouragement for our vocation with Scripture at the center of each reflection. Universal and useful at every level of education, this powerful, Spirit-led resource proves it's a good day to be a teacher."

—**Nick Smedal**, MA, Director of Spiritual Life and Theology Teacher, Living Word Lutheran High, Jackson, WI

IT'S A
Good Day
TO BE A
TEACHER

52 DEVOTIONS TO
EQUIP AND ENCOURAGE
EDUCATORS

GRETCHEN HUESMANN

Birmingham, Alabama

It's a Good Day to Be a Teacher

Iron Stream
An imprint of Iron Stream Media
100 Missionary Ridge
Birmingham, AL 35242
IronStreamMedia.com

Copyright © 2025 by Gretchen Huesmann

All rights reserved.

No part of this publication may be reproduced, stored in a retrieval system, or transmitted in any form or by any means—electronic, mechanical, photocopying, recording, or otherwise—without the prior written permission of the publisher.

Iron Stream Media serves its authors as they express their views, which may not express the views of the publisher. Although based on true events, the narratives and names in these devotions have been altered for privacy. All first-person stories reflect the actual experiences of the author.

Library of Congress Control Number: 2024940859

All Scripture quotations, unless otherwise indicated, are taken from the Holy Bible, New International Version®, NIV®. Copyright ©1973, 1978, 1984, 2011 by Biblica, Inc.™ Used by permission of Zondervan. All rights reserved worldwide. www.zondervan.com The "NIV" and "New International Version" are trademarks registered in the United States Patent and Trademark Office by Biblica, Inc.™

The Holy Bible, Berean Standard Bible, BSB is produced in cooperation with Bible Hub, Discovery Bible, OpenBible.com, and the Berean Bible Translation Committee. This text of God's Word has been dedicated to the public domain.

Scripture quotations are from the ESV® Bible (The Holy Bible, English Standard Version®), © 2001 by Crossway, a publishing ministry of Good News Publishers. Used by permission. All rights reserved. The ESV text may not be quoted in any publication made available to the public by a Creative Commons license. The ESV may not be translated in whole or in part into any other language.

Scripture quotations marked (GNT) are from the Good News Translation in Today's English Version—Second Edition Copyright © 1992 by American Bible Society. Used by Permission.

Scripture quotations marked KJV are from The Authorized (King James) Version. Rights in the Authorized Version in the United Kingdom are vested in the Crown. Reproduced by permission of the Crown's patentee, Cambridge University Press.

Scripture quotations marked NASB are taken from the (NASB®) New American Standard Bible®, Copyright © 1960, 1971, 1977, 1995, 2020 by The Lockman Foundation. Used by permission. All rights reserved. lockman.org

Scripture quotations marked NKJV are taken from the New King James Version®. Copyright © 1982 by Thomas Nelson. Used by permission. All rights reserved.

Scripture quotations marked (NLT) are taken from the *Holy Bible*, New Living Translation, copyright © 1996, 2004, 2015 by Tyndale House Foundation. Used by permission of Tyndale House Publishers, Carol Stream, Illinois 60188. All rights reserved.

Cover design by Hannah Linder Designs

ISBN: 978-1-56309-729-4 (paperback)
ISBN: 978-1-56309-738-6 (ebook)

1 2 3 4 5—29 28 27 26 25

*To my children, Timothy, Amanda, Aaron, and Grace.
Although you were not my first students, you will forever be my favorites.
Today, each of you impacts the lives of young people
in and out of the classroom.
Thank you for making a difference.*

*To my husband, Bernie. When we met at the onset of my teaching career, you promised an adventure and did not disappoint. From mountain peaks to sandy shores, there is no one I'd rather share this journey with than you.
Thank you for believing in me.*

*To my mother, Doris Jean Walther-Conrad. You were my first teacher and instilled in me a passion for books and learning. Yet watching you serve others has been the greatest life lesson.
Thank you for exemplifying Jesus's love to everyone you meet.*

Contents

Introduction xi
Fall Term 1
   New Roster 3
   Fresh Start 5
   Police Protection or God's Protection? 7
   Homeless 9
   Christ in Any Classroom 11
   He Knows Every Hair and Every Need 13
   Colleagues or Competitors? 15
   Actions and Words 17
   Contentment 19
   Go and Tell 21
   A Disastrous Day 23
   The Toughest Class Yet 25
   Unexpected Thanks 27
Winter Term 29
   Failure or Favored 31
   The Day I Became a Boys' PE Teacher 33
   Christmas Wonder 35
   Supernatural Strength 37
   Love and Pray 39
   Audible Witness 41
   Jesus, Help Me 43
   Each One Is a Gift 45
   "Jesus People" 47
   Storytelling 49
   Christ's Lunch Lesson 51
   Sunday Preparations 53
   When We Blow It 55

Contents

Spring Term 57
   The Power of a Picture 59
   Fighting Insecurity. 61
   School Unity 63
   Swarming. 65
   Fifty-Six More Days. 67
   The Workers Are Few 69
   Wardrobe Malfunction 71
   Show the Glow. 73
   The Great Protector. 75
   A Steady Race 77
   There's a Snake in Our School!. 79
   Mary Had a Little Goat. 81
   A Final Blessing 83

Summer Term 85
   Used Up. 87
   Joy Lost and Found 89
   Uprooted 91
   "I Can" Statement 93
   Independence. 95
   A Time for Everything. 97
   Donut Encounter 99
   Summer Surrender 101
   Unexpected Storm 103
   Sabbath Saboteurs 105
   Will I Teach Again? 107
   Eternal Education 109
   Walking in Tandem 111
   Topical Index. 113
   Acknowledgments 115
   About the Author. 116

Introduction

Sitting among my students during free play, I heard these words, "It's a good day to be a teacher." I blinked at the four-year-old who pressed her fingers into pink clay. "What did you just say?" I asked. Without looking up, the child repeated, "It's a good day to be a teacher."

I couldn't quite agree.

Like most teachers, on this first day back from break, I longed for yesterday's pajamas and coffee until noon. She grabbed a cookie cutter and added, "Someday, I want to be a teacher." Like the butterflies she shaped, her words floated around my head and settled in my heart.

My little friend was unaware that more than three hundred thousand teachers have left the profession since 2020.[1] She couldn't comprehend that educators have the highest rate of burnout.[2] Even if this beautiful child grows up to be a teacher, she will never know how much education has changed in recent years.

Still, somehow, I knew she spoke truth. It *is* a good day to be a teacher. Isn't it?

You know the answer if you continue to show up five days a week. You also understand and experience the growing challenges. So how do we survive? How can educators continue to fight the good fight in the classroom?

---

[1] Kathryn Dill, "School's Out for Summer and Many Teachers Are Calling It Quits," *The Wall Street Journal*, June 20, 2022, https://www.wsj.com/articles/schools-out-for-summer-and-many-teachers-are-calling-it-quits-11655732689.

[2] Stephanie Marken and Sangeeta Agrawal, "K-12 Workers Have Highest Burnout Rate in U.S." *Gallup News*, June 13, 2022, https://news.gallup.com/poll/393500/workers-highest-burnout-rate.aspx.

Introduction

First—whether we work in a public or parochial setting—we remember that "our struggle is not against flesh and blood, but against the rulers, against the authorities, against the powers of this dark world and against the spiritual forces of evil in the heavenly realms" (Ephesians 6:12). We may feel at war with our students, their parents, or our coworkers, but the Bible warns us of an enemy who strives to weaken our efforts and to kill and destroy (John 10:10; 1 Peter 5:8).

Second, since the battles we face involve unseen armies, we must prepare by putting on the full armor of God and using the sword of the Spirit, God's Word with prayer (Ephesians 6:17–19).

Maximizing This Devotional

Included with each devotion are four additional elements.

- **Read Aloud:** *Read out loud* the assigned verses, dedicating the space for God's work by speaking scripture in your empty classroom.
- **Pray Aloud:** *Pray out loud* over the empty seats before students arrive, inviting the Holy Spirit into lessons, learning, and relationships.
- **Live the Lesson:** Use suggested strategies for practical application.
- **Extra Credit:** Dive deeper into the Bible to nurture and fortify your faith.

Through these devotions and activities, you partner with God, who commissions our work and joins us in the classroom. I pray you will be encouraged, strengthened, and equipped each week.

Friend, with God's help, it *is* a good day to be a teacher.

Fall Term

While the stories of our schools may vary in their attractiveness, hopefulness, and effectiveness, all of us, together, collectively inhabit these stories.

—Lynn Swaner and Andy Wolfe, *Flourishing Together*

New Roster

Read Aloud Matthew 19:14

Let the little children come to me, and do not hinder them, for the kingdom of heaven belongs to such as these.

The teacher avoided his school email until the first day of August. After all, the next ten months would be nothing but work, which included sorting countless emails. Yet there was one missive he welcomed: the new roster. He looked forward to creating new name tags and locker labels. He also wondered, *Will you-know-who be in my room?* He knew the distribution of class assignments marked the beginning of a new community bringing friendships, laughter, and—like any ordinary family—disturbances, dislikes, and even dysfunction.

Indeed, a new school year includes a mix of personalities, backgrounds, and behaviors. Like a strange blend of ingredients, each student adds his or her own flavor and texture to the group. Yet God places every student in our lives and our classrooms for a purpose.

As Jesus was teaching and healing in front of large crowds (Matthew 19:2), small children were brought forward to be blessed, but his disciples "rebuked them" (19:13). Why did the children's presence bother the disciples? Was it their age? Their clothing? The Bible doesn't reveal the answer, only that Jesus did not refuse this latest "list of students." In fact, he welcomed and blessed them.

Before tackling the to-do list, begin by praying over your class list. Pray for each student, for their families, and for the friendships they will develop. Ask for the ability to welcome them as Christ does, with love, patience, and wisdom. No matter what names appear on your list, God has set this group before you and said, "These are my beloved children. I am entrusting them to your care."

Pray Aloud
Father, thank you for every student I will encounter this year. Give me wisdom and strength to challenge their minds, nurture their spirits, and affirm their value. Help me lead them to you so that their faith can flourish. Amen.

Live the Lesson
Begin praying for your class. Each time you type, write, or display their names, say a prayer on their behalf.

Extra Credit
Read Matthew 19:13–14 and John 3:16. Insert each student's name: "For God so loved [insert name] . . ."

Fresh Start

Read Aloud Isaiah 43:19

See, I am doing a new thing!
Now it springs up; do you not perceive it?
I am making a way in the wilderness
and streams in the wasteland.

"You'll be moving to room eight," the principal announced. Dread and disappointment filled the teacher. She closed her eyes, remembering all the visuals her classroom walls contained. She had to take everything down, only to be rehung. The supplies, books, and mounds of materials had to be boxed, hauled, unpacked, and reorganized. School started in four days.

This has likely happened to you. I know it has happened to me. A last-minute room change means a ton of work in a short amount of time.

However, a change in location can also provide a fresh start. When we've worked in the same room and the same grade, we develop a status quo, which can lead to stagnation and stale teaching. A different room can bring a new perspective, causing us to examine our environment and improve our strategies. Perhaps the incoming class will require a modified approach. Maybe the new space will be more conducive to their learning.

The change may have nothing to do with your practices or students. Perhaps God orchestrated the change for you to be near a less experienced teacher who needs encouragement.

Though his intentions may remain a mystery, he invites us to wait and see. In Isaiah 43:18–19, he tells us,

> Forget the former things;
>   do not dwell on the past.
> See, I am doing a new thing!
>   Now it springs up; do you not perceive it?
> I am making a way in the wilderness
>   and streams in the wasteland.

Though our flesh resists change and the work that accompanies it, we can trust in God's plan. He will use our new circumstances for his greater purposes.

Pray Aloud
Lord of All, I am grateful that nothing you do goes to waste. Thank you for the space where I can do your work. Use it and me for your glory and honor. Amen.

Live the Lesson
Whether you move classrooms this year or stay put, dedicate your space or office to God, asking him to bless the teaching, learning, and relationships that will grow within its walls.

Extra Credit
Read Isaiah 43. List new ways in which God is working in your life.

Police Protection or God's Protection?

Read Aloud 1 Samuel 17:45

David said to the Philistine, "You come against me with sword and spear and javelin, but I come against you in the name of the LORD Almighty, the God of the armies of Israel, whom you have defied."

Our staff gathered for professional development meetings in the lower-level library. The tables provided space for our large group, and the basement room offered relief from the August heat. The outer hallways formed a square around the perimeter of the library.

One late-summer morning, we began our meeting as usual except for a surprising announcement from our principal, "Our local police will be training in our building for an armed intruder drill." All morning long, fully equipped men and women in uniform radioed orders, raced, and ducked past the library doors while we discussed our classroom procedures for this modern-day danger.

The Israelites faced a new danger too: the Philistine giant, Goliath. He appeared in heavy armor and taunted Israel's army, intimidating them all—from the king to the water carrier. They had forgotten God's promise to be with them in battle. They had placed their trust in human size, weapons, and military strength rather than God. When David entered the camp and heard the threatening words, he was shocked at their fear and offered to fight Goliath himself. Rejecting King Saul's offer of armor, David boldly and successfully faced the enemy.

The debates continue about gun laws and police presence at educational institutions. The continuing threat of violence demands ongoing discussion. However, be assured, like David, we do not face danger alone. Our Almighty God—creator of the universe, separator of seas, and slayer of armies—can and will continue to fight for us.

Pray Aloud
Almighty Lord, guard and protect this school, its classrooms, and all who work and learn here. Keep danger far from this place. Surround our campus with your guardian angels. We put our trust in you. Amen.

Live the Lesson
Write the above prayer on a card. Add to it if desired. Pray the prayer aloud each day.

Extra Credit
Read Psalm 91. List the methods God uses to protect his people.

Homeless

Read Aloud Matthew 8:20 (ESV)

And Jesus said to him, "Foxes have holes, and birds of the air have nests, but the Son of Man has nowhere to lay his head."

My list of students sat before me with appointment dates next to each name, except for one. Dialing again, I sent up a quick prayer for success. To my surprise, a woman answered. After introducing myself as her child's new teacher, I began to explain the reason for my call. "A home visit will help me get acquainted with you and your child," I explained. "Sitting on the porch is an option too."

"You don't understand," the mom answered. "We have no home."

Although common during my early years of teaching, home visits have become quite rare. In a culture that reveres privacy, people today do not open their home to just anybody, especially a stranger. Yet meeting school families in their home provides a wonderful opportunity to build a relationship with them. I expected a few families to turn down my offer but never anticipated a homeless situation.

Jesus was homeless as well. Although the people crowded to hear his teaching and see his miracles, he was not welcome in his hometown. Many refused to listen, as he did not fulfill their expectations (Luke 4:16–30). Later, when a teacher of the law expressed a desire to follow Jesus, the Lord set him straight,

"The Son of Man has nowhere to lay his head." Jesus's explanation of homelessness spelled out the cost to follow him.

Following Jesus today has a cost as well, including disappointing people or not living a socially acceptable life or in a fancy neighborhood. When we pursue Christ, he might even lead us to unexpected places.

Eventually, I met the homeless child and his mom in a park and learned his father was in prison. They stayed with friends until his mother could secure another job. Our meeting provided opportunities to serve this family during the school year, in Christ's name.

Pray Aloud
Jesus, I thank you for leading me. Thank for you giving me the opportunity to share your love with my students. Open doors for me to witness and assist more in my community. It is a joy and privilege to follow you. Amen.

Live the Lesson
What do you know about your students? Even if you never visit their homes or meet their parents, a few well-placed questions might provide answers. Look for ways to quietly assist a family in need.

Extra Credit
Read Matthew 8. Reflect on the possible thoughts and feelings of those who witnessed Christ's actions in this chapter. How has following Jesus cost you? Then read Romans 8:18.

Christ in Any Classroom

Read Aloud Romans 8:9 (ESV)
You, however, are not in the flesh but in the Spirit, if in fact the Spirit of God dwells in you.

Several years ago, the parochial childcare center where I worked decided to partner with the local public school system to provide free four-year-old prekindergarten. Although not included in the curriculum, religious instruction would be allowed before and after school hours. The administration gave me the green light to invite our community families to learn about Jesus.

The thought of inviting every rostered family into this unique arrangement made my pulse race. *Would the parents laugh? Be offended?* Nervous about the school day, I wondered, *Will I have to hide my faith? Can I even do that?* With each step, I prayed for God to go with me.

And, of course, he did.

The Holy Spirit, who gives us faith, accompanies baptized believers of Christ everywhere. He goes with us into every home. He joins us in the classroom. Regardless of whether our schools exhibit crosses or display Bible verses, the living God, when invited, is present.

What a joy to know we do not teach alone! What an honor to take Jesus out into our communities, whether to parks, to shopping malls, to schools, or to wherever else he leads us.

Some may have viewed the partnership with a public school system as a compromise in our beliefs. However, our Christian organization recognized the opportunity to bring Jesus to the neighborhood children and their families. Indeed, whether we teach in a parochial or public setting, when we have the indwelling of the Holy Spirit, we bring Christ with us.

Pray Aloud

Be present in this classroom, Lord. Work powerfully here to draw all who enter closer to you. Let your love shine through me so that others can know you too. Amen.

Live the Lesson

Each day, invite God to join you in your classroom. When you leave, remember he is going with you. Carry a small object—a cross, a rock, or some other item—to remind you of God's continuous presence.

Extra Credit

Read Romans 8. List the benefits of having the Holy Spirit in us.

He Knows Every Hair and Every Need

Read Aloud Luke 12:7

Indeed, the very hairs of your head are all numbered. Don't be afraid; you are worth more than many sparrows.

He walked into my classroom like any newcomer, his brown eyes darting from the dangling ceiling art to the poster-clad walls. His smileless face avoided mine as well as the curious looks of his new classmates. What his countenance hid, his lengthy Individualized Education Program (IEP) revealed: a trauma-filled experience followed by relearning almost every life skill and then rejection from his family. The wounds he'd endured involved the heart and mind as much as the body.

The number of troubled students has risen greatly over the last decades. In my early years of teaching, I had one or two special cases that would enter my room roughly every other year. Today, we are hard-pressed to find enough workers to support the needs of our classrooms.

Luke reminds us today that Jesus thoroughly comprehends the depth of each student's needs. He understands how their brain computes. He knows the exact care required to mend broken hearts and wounded souls. His love exceeds all past, present, and future suffering.

Although we regular teachers need support from our special education colleagues, as do our students, let us not forget to call upon the One who knows our classes the best. He provides wisdom, strength, and insight to those who ask.

For this newest student, the wisdom included saying goodbye and entrusting more equipped educators to nurture him. But I will never forget this child's face; indeed, his picture reminds me that although I cannot be his long-term educator, I can pray daily for him.

Pray Aloud

Jesus, you are the one who created each person who enters my class. You know all their needs and the best ways to educate them. Give me wisdom to effectively guide, teach, and nurture every precious student. Amen.

Live the Lesson

Consider your most challenging students. Are you praying regularly for them? Do you need more support to provide for their needs? Take your concerns to the One who knows what's best for your students.

Extra Credit

Read Luke 12:22–33. Look for ways Jesus cares for his own. What promises does he make in these verses?

Colleagues or Competitors?

Read Aloud Proverbs 27:17
*As iron sharpens iron,
so one person sharpens another.*

The teachers gathered for another professional development day.

"I'll be visiting all the classrooms," the administrator shared.

A collective moan emanated from the group.

"In time, you will visit one another's classes across the district," she continued.

Some teachers looked confused by this. "Why?" one whispered to a colleague. "We don't have time for observations."

As if reading their minds, the principal added, "Our goal is to work collaboratively and learn from one another. Sharing our collective experiences and practices will sharpen our skills."

A dull knife is still a knife. Left isolated, its sharpness wanes. However, rubbing two knives together improves the efficiency and effectiveness of both.

We see this truth played out by New Testament Christians as described in the book of Acts. These early believers gathered to learn, pray, and worship despite intense persecution. They shared stories of God's wonderful work, offering encouragement to one another, and the first Christian churches blossomed.

The same holds true for us in the teaching profession. When engaged in mutual learning and idea sharing, we not only enhance our skills but cultivate a more favorable learning environment for our students.

However, some take a more reticent approach and prefer to keep to themselves. Others reject new ideas or resist change. Yet today's proverb establishes God's design for relational learning and edification, which requires an open mindset and willingness to share our gifts. Never underestimate the value of mutual learning to keep our minds and skills sharp.

Pray Aloud

Dear Lord, do I have an open mind to continue to learn, or is it closed to new techniques? Help me not become complacent in my learning but be willing to gain new insights and share my expertise with others who may benefit. Amen.

Live the Lesson

If you have never participated in peer observations, discuss the possibility with your school. Once- or twice-a-year visits to similar grade levels can provide valuable information and allow for growth for all participants.

Extra Credit

Read Acts 2:42–47. Why did the believers meet regularly? What did they talk about?

Actions and Words

Read Aloud 2 Corinthians 9:13

Because of the service by which you have proved yourselves, others will praise God for the obedience that accompanies your confession of the gospel of Christ, and for your generosity in sharing with them and with everyone else.

Just before school let out for the day, a parent entered the restroom and found herself privy to a discussion between two women. Their conversation volleyed over the bathroom stall walls uninterrupted:

"Did you see what she posted yesterday?" said one.

"I did. How disgusting. And she talks like such a church girl," said the other.

"I'm ready to hide her after what she said to my kid last week."

"You can hide her online, but you'll still see her face in church each week."

"Ugh. I know!"

The chatter continued as the uninvolved listener took mental note: *if this is how Christians behave, I want nothing to do with it.*

Gossip existed as much in the first century as it does today, despite the absence of social media. People slandered Paul's name and questioned his testimony of Christ—all without social media platforms, television, or newspapers. Paul's character often came into question, given his past attacks on the earliest believers. Church folks and heathens alike watched his movements and compared them to his preaching and teaching.

Similarly, others observe us—our reactions to stress, our social media posts—and compare our actions to our words. Do our activities align with our beliefs? If not, our testimony of faith falls short. Of course, we don't do this perfectly. Paul owned up to his shortcomings as "chief of sinners" (1 Timothy 1:15 KJV). As Christ's ambassadors, we confess, forgive, and reconcile to mirror God's grace through Jesus.

The gossiping women were unaware of how their words affected the unintentional listener. But the enemy understood. The devil will use our behavior against Christ's cause. Let's be certain our actions and words build Christ's kingdom, not tear it down.

Pray Aloud

Gracious Lord, keep a guard over my mouth today that I may not say anything to thwart your work. Let my words be filled with love and grace and my actions reflect my faith in you. Amen.

Live the Lesson

We teach our students to be kind, respectful, and loving. How can we model that this week? Watch for opportunities to walk the talk.

Extra Credit

Read 2 Corinthians 9. Note Paul's observations of the Corinthian Christians. How did he call out their Christian witness? What does that mean for us?

Contentment

Read Aloud 1 Timothy 6:6

But godliness with contentment is great gain.

Halfway through the first quarter, the sixth-grade students had established "their spots" in the cafeteria. They coughed, cackled, and blushed their way through the lunch hour. Boys huddled near boys, and girls sat near one another, with the occasional mix across the table. Then, *it* happened.

A pink-faced boy glanced toward a pretty blonde sitting kitty-corner from him, "Will you be my girlfriend?" he squeaked.

The girl looked straight into his flushed face and replied, "No. I like frogs."

Thus rejected, the blushing boy turned his attention to his ham sandwich.

Oh, that we could have the confidence of that bright girl! What joy we'd experience with such contentment. Great is the temptation to constantly look toward the next season of life.

When Timothy penned the words in our verse, he addressed slaves, not sixth graders or twenty-first-century educators. He urged his readers, even in their low position, to seek godliness over wealth or position and warned them of coveting more.

Similarly, the enemy tempts us to ponder what we might be missing. If the grass seems greener at another school or you're tempted by more money and the promise of happiness, the enemy may dwell in those thoughts.

When we seek godliness rather than rush to the next stage or long for something beyond our grasp, we gain far more than that which lures us.

The confident middle-school girl knew what she wanted. The chuckles that followed her refusal did not faze her. In her firm yet funny way, she communicated her message to all the boys that day: "I'm not interested in having a boyfriend yet. I'm content to be a kid."

Pray Aloud
Lord, open my eyes to the blessings around me. When my heart feels as if it's missing out, remind me of my current calling and fill my heart with joy. Amen.

Live the Lesson
Which blessings in your life do you take for granted? Create a list of the necessities such as clothing, food, and transportation God has given you. Include all the positive features of your current school. Add your family, friends, and, of course, Jesus to the list.

Extra Credit
Read 1 Timothy 6. What strategies does Paul suggest for maintaining a grateful heart?

Go and Tell

Read Aloud Mark 16:15

He said to them, "Go into all the world and preach the gospel to all creation."

"Why do you even do Show-and-Tell?" one parent complained. "My child does not like to speak in front of his friends. In fact, neither do I! Give me one good reason why I should make him."

The teacher nodded in agreement. The woman's child had hardly uttered two words the entire school year. She was concerned about the boy's shyness. "Show-and-Tell gives him an opportunity to practice," the teacher said. "Having him say a few words in our classroom setting will help his confidence grow. You'll see, when he brings a favorite item that he's excited about, the words will come."

I wonder what Jesus's disciples thought when they first heard the commission to go and preach. Were they nervous? Did they feel prepared? Many had heard and witnessed his authoritative sermons then were sent out in pairs (Mark 6:7). Were they ready to go and tell? After his death and resurrection, Jesus instructed his disciples to wait in Jerusalem until the Holy Spirit came on them (Acts 1:4). Ready or not, the Holy Spirit's power provided any boldness and confidence they may have been lacking.

What about us? Do we share the gospel with confidence? Or does talking about Jesus still get caught in our throats while our hearts pound? Christ's provision for his followers is our source of courage too. We can ask for the same Holy Spirit to speak through us and give us the ability to clearly communicate God's message of hope.

Additionally, just like in the case of our shy young friend, practice helps. The more we witness and share our story of God's work in our lives, the easier the words flow from our lips. We can show and tell his love to all we meet.

Pray Aloud
Holy Spirit, fill me today with strength and power that I may be a witness of your love. Provide opportunities for me to share your good news here and wherever I go. Amen.

Live the Lesson
Has God placed someone in your life who doesn't know about him? Pray for an opportunity to witness.

Extra Credit
Read John 18:15–18 and Acts 2:1–41. Compare and contrast Peter's witness in both situations. What made the difference in his later testimony?

A Disastrous Day

Read Aloud Lamentations 3:22–23

Because of the Lord's great love we are not consumed,
 for his compassions never fail.
They are new every morning;
 great is your faithfulness.

I lost a child today. No, not by death. One sneaky student slipped away as we returned to the classroom after a bathroom break. Misplacing a child is never good. But on this day, an administrator, present for evaluations, observed my disastrous day. With a red face and pounding heart, I alerted my assistant. Thankfully, he found the missing pupil hiding near the restroom. Relieved but frustrated, I envisioned an F for failure on the observer's clipboard.

All educators experience disastrous days on occasion that threaten our confidence and sap our patience. Tempted to replay those events in our minds, we relive all the feelings of failure and long for a restart.

In the book of Lamentations, Jeremiah describes one dreadful day after another. Like us, he recalls each event, describing the destruction of Jerusalem and remembering every emotion. Then in chapter 3 we read,

> Yet this I call to mind
> and therefore I have hope:
> Because of the Lord's great love we are not consumed,
> for his compassions never fail.
> They are new every morning. (vv. 21–23)

These words remind us that we must release the past so we can grasp tomorrow's hope.

Thank God for his great love and grace, which covers every disaster! Though such moments threaten to defeat us, they cannot. Each new day brings a fresh beginning. Like a clean board at the morning bell, God forgives us and offers unending compassion and mercy for whatever we face. Unlike my patience with the sly student, God's love never wears out. We receive a fresh dose with each dawn.

Pray Aloud
Heavenly Father, thank you for your unending love. Help me place the past in your hands and be as compassionate with my students—and myself—as you are. Amen.

Live the Lesson
Each time you erase your board, remember the fresh start we are given through Christ's death and resurrection.

Extra Credit
Read Psalm 103 this week. Reflect on Christ's redeeming love and forgiveness.

The Toughest Class Yet

Read Aloud Psalm 139:13
For you created my inmost being;
  you knit me together in my mother's womb.

The baffled teacher threw up his hands. He had tried everything! By October, he dubbed this group "The Toughest Class Yet." In his search for solutions, he wondered, *Were they extra energetic or hyperactive? Disobedient or distracted?* To be fair, the environment was far from ideal. With no windows, bathroom, or even a sink in the classroom, he labored to create a welcoming atmosphere in the cramped, dark space. He did his best to set up colorful bulletin boards and inviting spaces. Class rules had been taught, modeled, and reinforced. Still, several boys, and a girl or two, created daily mayhem. Even the consistent use of calming, classical melodies couldn't reduce their energy.

So he did what any smart educator would do: he asked for help. Not from administrators, colleagues, or parents, for those had also been tried. This time he grabbed his list of students and headed to the nearby chapel. Before the first bus arrived, he talked to the One who created the individuals who confounded him.

Only God can unlock the mystery behind each personality who enters our classrooms. He sees the intricacies of their minds and understands their behaviors. He knows why Brandon arrived angry yesterday and why Katie often cries. We can go to the One who "knit them together" and ask for wisdom, insight, and strength.

But let's not seek God as a last resort. Why not begin each school year—indeed, each day—praying for our students. When we thank God for each one, we remember the great love Jesus has for them. We recall the God-given qualities and contributions they bring to our room. He imparts the insight needed to help them.

As the exasperated teacher discovered, when we bring our most difficult class before our Savior, he provides strength and wisdom to face another day. Who knows? The toughest group may transform into the best class yet.

Pray Aloud
Thank you, Lord, for each student I am privileged to serve. Show me how to share your love, and the methods needed to assist them in learning. Grant me patience to endure. Amen.

Live the Lesson
Which students concern you the most? Next to each name on your class list, write one positive attribute they possess.

Extra Credit
Read Psalm 139. Reflect on God's thorough knowledge of your students and you.

Unexpected Thanks

Read Aloud Luke 17:15-16 (NASB)
Now one of them, when he saw that he had been healed, turned back, glorifying God with a loud voice, and he fell on his face at His feet, giving thanks to Him. And he was a Samaritan.

The teacher held an envelope and searched for a return address. Finding none, he tore the envelope open and pulled out a hastily folded and wrinkled paper. He placed the paper on his desk and smoothed it with his palm.

"Dear Mr. Thomas," the note read. "I hope you remember me. You sent me to the office a million times; how could you forget? The last day it happened, I walked past the office and out the door. I hated you. I figured you hated me too. All I knew was hate." The letter continued with a description of the former student's stint in shoplifting and drugs, landing him in jail.

"Then a guy came and told me about Jesus," the letter continued. "He set the record straight on what love is and hate isn't. All that stuff you said and did—I didn't get it. I get it now. Anyway, thanks," signed S.J.

Most teachers have wondered, "Am I making a difference? Am I wasting my time?" The brief nine months with our students may result in academic progress and growth in maturity. Yet we can't help wondering whether our short-term association with our students produces long-term effects.

The man in today's verse crossed paths briefly with Jesus. After he and nine other outcasts sought the Lord for healing, Jesus responded by sending them away with an assignment, "Go and show yourselves to the priests" (17:14 NASB).

Notice their healing did not occur immediately. Only after they departed did the men see their skin restored. Their quick interlude with Jesus changed their lives forever. Cured of the painful skin disease, the men returned to their families and society. Afterward, only one remembered to go back and thank the Healer.

We know most students will never express gratitude to us, and it is likely that the full impact of our efforts will remain a mystery this side of heaven. However, we can trust that, with God's help, our brief time with our students will have long-lasting effects. Let's not forget to thank God for his work in us and in our students.

Pray Aloud
Lord, thank you for all you have done in my life. Despite my fear and failings, work in and through me for your glory. Amen.

Live the Lesson
Who made a difference in your own life? It may not be too late to send a note of thanks.

Extra Credit
Read Psalm 118. The Psalms are like thank-you notes to the Lord. Compose a psalm in gratitude to him.

Winter Term

Although we can pray in our hearts without saying anything aloud, words and gestures help kindle the spirit. So our entire lives should be devoted to God—spreading his Word and praising his kingdom. Whatever we do must be grounded in sincere prayer.

—Martin Luther, *Faith Alone*

Failure or Favored

Read Aloud 1 John 3:1 (NKJV)

Behold what manner of love the Father has bestowed on us, that we should be called children of God!

"It's not working. Nothing I tried with my students today brought success," the young teacher said.

The mentor handed her a tissue and then replied, "When they didn't get it, how did that make you feel?"

"Their failure made me feel like a failure. Like I can't do this. Did I miss my call? Should I be doing something else?"

A world like ours, focused on achievement and advancement, expects success. For some, failure is not an option. We praise the best grades and the highest ratings and condemn minimal efforts and barely passing scores. We expect success from our students. We expect it from ourselves. And then when a lesson turns disastrous, our focus turns inward, attacking our self-esteem and casting doubt on our abilities.

Recognizing and rewarding accomplishments have their place as long as we do not misrepresent personal value as defined by our works. Our worth has little to do with our achievements and everything to do with who we are and to whom we belong. Our Father in heaven showers love upon us as his beloved children. Any work involved in this bond was accomplished for us by Christ's death on the cross. His atonement for our sin deems us worthy without any effort on our part.

The young teacher's mentor asked one more question of her, "What would you tell a student who is failing your class?"

The teacher smiled. "I would remind them they are not defined by their grades, good or bad."

Pray Aloud

Lord, you love me with a deep and abiding love, not for any work on my part, but only because you created me and made me your child. Help me share that same depth of love with my students. Amen.

Live the Lesson

Listen to your language this week as you praise your students. How often is achievement involved? Find ways to honor students for who they are rather than what they do.

Extra Credit

Read 1 John 3 and 4. Ponder the truths we learn about love in these chapters.

The Day I Became a Boys' PE Teacher

Read Aloud 2 Corinthians 12:9

But he said to me, "My grace is sufficient for you, for my power is made perfect in weakness." Therefore I will boast all the more gladly about my weaknesses, so that Christ's power may rest on me.

They called him Coach Jefferson. The physical education teacher's large frame and athletic build garnered the respect of unruly junior high boys without a word. But on this day, he'd fallen victim to whatever virus coursed through the school and asked me to substitute for him.

"You know, I teach mostly young children," I texted.

"Yep," he replied.

"And I'm female."

"LOL. Yes."

He must be desperate, I thought. "OK, I'll come, but give me detailed lesson plans and classroom management tips," I pleaded.

As I drove toward the school, I realized the sweat on my brow had nothing to do with the Florida heat. As a substitute, I knew the confidence required to step into a classroom. *Lord, I have zero ability to face a gym full of junior high boys!* I had nothing to draw upon for this assignment except all the negative little-girl feelings from my own past. Facing junior high boys equaled facing Goliath.

God often appointed difficult tasks to his people. From Genesis to Revelation, we witness God-ordained assignments given to men and women who felt the same trepidation and disqualification. Most, if not all, expressed the same sentiments: "Help! I can't do this!" Each time, God's answered, "I have you right where I want you. With my power, you can do anything." Our God, who multiplied meager loaves and fishes, receives our small efforts and transforms them into God-sized accomplishments.

I am happy to report I survived PE that day. In fact, I subbed for Coach Jefferson several times after, but only with God's grace and power.

Pray Aloud
Lord, I need your power to accomplish your will. When I feel weak, remind me of your strength. When I feel small, let me recall how big and wide are your love and provision for me. Amen.

Live the Lesson
In what ways do you foster confidence in your students? What strategies can you apply in your own life?

Extra Credit
Read 2 Corinthians 12. Study Paul's struggles and his suggestions for dealing with them.

Christmas Wonder

Read Aloud Luke 2:20

The shepherds returned, glorifying and praising God for all the things they had heard and seen, which were just as they had been told.

A teacher retold the Christmas story in religion class, trying to ignore the blank stares of his students. He asked intermittent questions to keep their attention. *They've heard this a million times*, he thought. Then he noticed the intent gaze of one girl in the back. She had recently transferred from the public school. Although she usually doodled in a notebook, this day she looked at the teacher as if intently listening.

When the teacher shared about Gabriel's visit to Joseph, the girl's hand shot up. "What did he do?" she asked. "Did Joseph divorce her or what?"

For a moment no one moved. The teacher and the remaining students stared at the newcomer, realizing this classmate was hearing these details for the first time. The teacher continued with renewed vigor.

For those raised in the church, we take these familiar stories for granted. We often assume others have heard what we have been taught. The familiar story of Christ's birth, when read year after year, becomes commonplace to us. That is, until we experience the Christmas wonder through the eyes of someone learning of it for the first time.

I am curious if the shepherds' families and friends grew tired of hearing their account. Did they stare in boredom each time the men recounted the angel's words or glorious singing? Did the shepherds lose enthusiasm over their experience with the passage of time?

We'd like to think not, but the Bible doesn't say. In fact, we never hear of these specific shepherds again. Yet we know their story. Retold each year, their witness of the baby Jesus and all the components of the Christmas event cause us to wonder, rejoice, and share with the same enthusiasm of those lowly visitors who beheld the Son of God.

Pray Aloud

Jesus, I marvel at your birth and all the circumstances surrounding that period. Give me the same bold joy the shepherds expressed to recount the story with wonder and awe. Amen.

Live the Lesson

Look for opportunities to share the joy of Christmas with someone who may not have heard.

Extra Credit

Read Luke 2. Reflect, ponder, and wonder at the Christmas events and miraculous details.

Supernatural Strength

Read Aloud Isaiah 40:28-29
Do you not know?
Have you not heard?
The Lord is the everlasting God,
the Creator of the ends of the earth.
He will not grow tired or weary,
and his understanding no one can fathom.
He gives strength to the weary
and increases power of the weak.

The car line wrapped around the coffee shop, tempting me to forgo the coveted beverage. I had saved a gift card for this first morning after the break, knowing I might long for a special treat to face the post-holiday classroom. *Just be patient*, I thought. Joining the queue, I considered my order. Would an extra shot of espresso ease the transition? Would the wait be worth it? Maybe, maybe not. Though my classroom and lesson plans sat ready and waiting, my emotional preparedness waned. Caffeine might help, yet I knew only supernatural strength could meet the need.

Whenever we take a break, such as a work holiday or a pause from our routine, we often lack motivation to restart, regardless of how rested we feel. On these days, when energy eludes us, let us not forget the Source of all power and strength.

The Creator of the universe, who never wearies, stands ready to provide his power to those who cry out to him. The Bible assures us God understands. He modeled and instituted the Sabbath rest. He welcomes our weakness and offers to meet even our energy needs. Our fatigue presents an opportunity for us to rely on him and receive his strength to face the day and the classroom. The best part is, there are no long lines and no gift cards required. We need only ask.

Pray Aloud
Powerful and Almighty God, when I feel exceptionally tired and unmotivated to tackle the tasks before me, I ask for strength and energy. Equip me to be an effective servant and share your love through my words and actions. Amen.

Live the Lesson
Write the Isaiah verses out on a card. Place the card in a conspicuous area such as your car or classroom desk. Commit this section of scripture to memory and draw on God's strength when weariness returns.

Extra Credit
Read Isaiah 40. List examples of God's strength from this chapter.

Love and Pray

Read Aloud Matthew 5:44

But I tell you, love your enemies and pray for those who persecute you.

After being reprimanded by her teacher, a student fired back, "Why don't you just quit! You're making things worse here." The stunned teacher stared at her young pupil. The child was only seven years old.

Jesus commanded, "Love your enemies. Pray for those who persecute you." Who would have thought we would be applying that verse to our students? The harsh comments, death threats, and violence in many of today's schools leave us wondering if we work in a classroom or on a battlefield.

Yet if we focus only on the words *enemies* and *persecution*, we miss Christ's divine strategy: love and pray. When we bring our concerns for each student—for their mental, spiritual, and physical health—to the throne of our Savior, our love for them blossoms.

Additionally, through prayer, we engage in the real battle behind a student's threats or actions. Ephesians 6:12 reminds us, "Our struggle is not against flesh and blood, but against the rulers, against the authorities, against the powers of this dark world and against the spiritual forces of evil in the heavenly realms." God knows each student intimately, their story and their pain.

Certainly, the teacher grew thicker skin that day. She also wondered if perhaps the child had heard similar words before and lashed out in response to something unrelated to the classroom altogether. Such an empathetic reaction is to love. When we combine love with prayer, we join forces with the One who loves perfectly and fights all our battles.

Pray Aloud
Lord of heaven and earth, you know and love each young person in my care. Help me remember that my students and parents are not the enemy but your beloved children. Give me insight and understanding to the challenges they face and help me respond with patience and love. Amen.

Live the Lesson
Divide your roster of students into five groups. Each day pray for a different set of names, listing your educational concerns, any family issues you know about, and their relationships with one another.

Extra Credit
Read Matthew 5. Study Jesus's radical instructions for responding to our adversaries with love.

Audible Witness

Read Aloud Acts 16:25
About midnight Paul and Silas were praying and singing hymns to God, and the other prisoners were listening to them.

The snow started around noon. An hour into the afternoon training session, the leaders dismissed the teachers early so we could begin the trek home. Earlier in the day, my coworker and I had crossed our mountain pass under blue skies—not a flake in sight—to attend the mandatory training for our county's educators. Now, we raced back up the mountain hoping to beat the worst of the storm. As we ascended the mountain pass in my four-cylinder sedan, visibility decreased until whiteout conditions met us at the summit.

I gripped the steering wheel, and my prayers changed from silent pleas to verbal outcries.

"Please God, keep us on the road. Lord, protect us and open the way for us to get home."

My coworker clutched the passenger-side door in silence.

Peter and Silas faced a storm of their own. Thrown into prison for casting out an evil spirit, they had been stripped, beaten, and imprisoned with feet in shackles and under heavy guard. Their situation seemed hopeless, yet they responded with unabashed praying and singing. These faithful followers exhibited their total reliance on God to anyone who listened, including the guards and other prisoners. They looked past their pain, weakness, and miserable situation and put their faith in he who is unseen. They trusted his plan for their next days, even if they faced death.

When the foundations of the prison shook, those in attendance also knew and believed in the One who had received the sung and spoken prayers.

When danger looms or circumstances become desperate, let us boldly and outwardly cry out to the Lord. He hears us, and you never know who else may be listening.

As my colleague and I inched down the other side of the pass, the total white turned brighter and the snow lighter. By the time we reached our tiny town, the sun's rays peeked through the clouds.

"You really believe God did that, don't you?" my passenger asked.

"We're here, aren't we?" I chuckled, still a bit shaky. "My driving skills certainly didn't bring us home."

After dropping her at her house, I prayed again, "Lord, let her see you."

Pray Aloud

Heavenly Father, I pray right now for the safety of this school and all who enter it. Protect us and guide us through the day. Let no harm come to the teachers, students, or families. Amen.

Live the Lesson

Are you comfortable praying out loud? If not, practice by reciting the verse and prayers aloud as suggested in these devotions.

Extra Credit

Read Acts 16. How did God use the circumstances in this chapter to expand his kingdom?

Jesus, Help Me

Read Aloud Psalm 105:4-5

Look to the Lord and his strength;
seek his face always.
Remember the wonders he has done.

A student darted back and forth, leaping between bus seats and across the aisle. I glanced at his mom chatting with another parent behind her. The commotion caught her attention, but she ignored her son's activity, prompting my intervention. "Please sit down by your mom," I told the child. "It's not safe for you to be moving around."

You can probably guess what happened next. Embarrassed that I would scold her child in such a manner, the parent shot off an angry email to me and my administrator as soon as we returned from the field trip. Unfortunately, a subsequent meeting with the outraged parent failed to resolve the situation. When I prepared for a second appointment, this time with the mom and my principal, I distinctly remember praying, "Jesus, help me!" A peace fell over me like a warm blanket as I entered the conference room.

Today, before I meet with any parent, I invite God into the situation. Only he has the power to soften hearts and open eyes. Additionally, he provides me with the strength and the words to communicate effectively.

In Psalm 105, the Lord invites us to seek him always. Imagine his sympathetic countenance as you share your struggles with the Savior. Whatever we encounter—a struggling student, an angry parent, or a disgruntled coworker—we are not alone. God walks beside us through each day and each conflict. At any moment, we can call out to him, and he will answer.

There's no doubt my principal's presence contributed to the success of that final meeting. Yet I believe the fourth Attendee made all the difference.

Pray Aloud
Gracious Lord, you are Emmanuel, God with us. Thank you for your continual presence in our lives and your help in all circumstances. Amen.

Live the Lesson
Recall a time when God showed up exactly when you needed him. Post today's verse near your desk as a reminder to invite Jesus into all your struggles.

Extra Credit
Read Psalm 105. Underline all the verbs, every action made by the Lord. Ponder his mighty work.

Each One Is a Gift

Read Aloud Ephesians 4:11 (BSB)
It was He who gave some to be apostles, some to be prophets, some to be evangelists, and some to be pastors and teachers.

"Not again." Ted closed his email and sighed. His administrator called *another* staff meeting. The third one this week. "Doesn't she understand we have work to do?" he asked his empty classroom.

The new principal had annoyed him since she joined their faculty. Nothing like the trusting principal before, this one had her fingers in everything. Or so it seemed. Was she a micromanager? Ted hadn't decided yet.

Just as our classes include a blend of personalities, backgrounds, and learning styles, so too, our education teams contain a variety of leadership skills. Occasionally, those diversities clash, which can swiftly lead to dislike or even disrespect.

Instead of focusing on our differences, however, what if we saw each team member as bringing something unique to the table? Our verse reminds us that we are blessed to work alongside distinctive individuals with God-given gifts, even with members who may differ from us or with whom we disagree. That's the beauty of the varied talents God bestows on those he calls.

As Ted neared the meeting room, a coworker joined him. "She's a good communicator, isn't she?" his colleague asked, referring to the new principal. Ted couldn't help marveling at this completely different perspective.

Our differences can divide or strengthen our teams. Let us appreciate God's design and approach one another with respect and grace.

Pray Aloud
Lord, thank you for each person on our staff. When we differ, help me work with grace. Let me treat each colleague with the same unconditional love you have for us. Amen.

Live the Lesson
Can you identify specific talents and abilities your coworkers contribute to your staff? If not, ask God to show you.

Extra Credit
Read Ephesians 4:1–16 and 1 Corinthians 12. Consider how varied the body of Christ is. Note the gifts God gives.

"Jesus People"

Read Aloud Acts 5:41

The apostles left the Sanhedrin, rejoicing because they had been counted worthy of suffering disgrace for the Name.

Nathan sat in the breakroom eating lunch when a coworker entered and grabbed a cart full of supplies. "Now don't go telling our principal what you just saw," he warned. "I know how you 'Jesus people' like to rat us out."

Dumbfounded, Nathan stared at the other teacher. Taking more than the allotted classroom materials, although against the rules, was a minor offense. Running to the principal never occurred to Nathan. What bothered him more was this coworker's assumption that he would do so simply because of his Christianity. *Will I seem like a weak Christian now if I say nothing? Or will it be a better witness to call out the wrongdoing? Is it even my place? I feel like I'm the one in trouble now.* Nathan wrestled with these thoughts the rest of the day.

The early Christians often found themselves in trouble for their faith. Arrested, beaten, even jailed, the faith-filled believers suffered. Many were killed. Some had scattered at Jesus's arrest and trial and hid in fear after his death. They later boldly proclaimed Christ's redeeming work on the cross and rejoiced in the trouble heaped upon them for Jesus's sake.

What made the difference? What turned these cowering followers into confident witnesses? Everything changed at Pentecost when the Spirit of God transformed their weak faith into courageous testimonies. Their own humanness, their tendency to recoil from pain and trouble, remained the same. But the indwelling of the Holy Spirit strengthened them amid their difficulties. They recognized that their troubles resembled those of their Savior's and felt honored to suffer so.

By evening, Nathan had released the other teacher's conduct to the Lord and praised God because his coworker considered Nathan a "Jesus person."

Pray Aloud

Jesus, the agony you faced does not compare to my meager trials. By your Holy Spirit's power, strengthen my faith and my witness. Amen.

Live the Lesson

If you have not suffered recently for the gospel, pray for opportunities to move out of your comfort zone to share Jesus more. Trust that you do not go alone. The Holy Spirit will provide the needed courage and words.

Extra Credit

Read Acts 5. What were the early Christians willing to endure to grow God's kingdom?

Storytelling

Read Aloud 2 Samuel 12:1 (NLT)
So the Lord sent Nathan the prophet to tell David this story: "There were two men in a certain town. One was rich, and one was poor."

A mom sat across from Mrs. Lander, her daughter's teacher. "My child told me the same classmate has hit her every day this week!"

The teacher gasped, "Really? She said that?"

"Who is the bully, Mrs. Lander?" the mom demanded.

The teacher took a deep breath and said, "That's why I scheduled our meeting. I'm sorry, but your daughter has been doing the hitting, not the other way around. I'm afraid she's been telling you stories."

The prophet Nathan used the storytelling tactic to confront King David. The tale of the stolen sheep furnished David with perspective and empathy before Nathan shined a light on the king's adultery. A duly convicted King David repented of his sin.

Jesus, a master storyteller, often used parables. Understanding human defense mechanisms, he related everyday occurrences to instruct, explain, or convict his listeners. When we read his parables today, the images aid in our understanding and help us retain his truths.

God continues to use our daily experiences to teach us. Have you noticed? After the rain pours for five days in a row, we appreciate the sunshine. When difficulties arise, our answered prayers teach us to rely on the Lord. At the loss of a loved one, we learn the value of life.

The young child in Mrs. Lander's class may have been attempting to avoid punishment, but another possibility exists. Unable to admit her wrongdoing, she may have created a story to elicit aid in a stressful situation. In other words, her tale might have been a cry for help.

There are lessons to be learned from the stories of our students and those of our Lord. When we apply the Bible to narratives around us, we grow in wisdom, in empathy, and in our faith.

Pray Aloud

Dear God, open my eyes to what you are trying to teach me. Speak to me through your Word and strengthen my faith. Amen.

Live the Lesson

No matter your age group, stories enhance our teaching. Look for ways to bring parables, fables, and allegorical methods into your lessons this week.

Extra Credit

Read Luke 8. How did Jesus use these parables and situations to teach life lessons?

Christ's Lunch Lesson

Read Aloud Matthew 9:10-12
While Jesus was having dinner at Matthew's house, many tax collectors and sinners came and ate with him and his disciples. When the Pharisees saw this, they asked his disciples, "Why does your teacher eat with tax collectors and sinners?" On hearing this, Jesus said, "It is not the healthy who need a doctor, but the sick."

A girl glanced at her new classmates, lunch tray in hand. When no one invited her to join them, she found an empty place near the end.

"Why doesn't she just sit with them?" one adult complained out of earshot. The teachers had a clear view from their table and quickly sized up the situation.

"She acts a little stuck up," another chimed in. "She came from New York, you know."

One brave teacher cleared her throat and countered, "The girl just moved here, and you expect her to sit with them uninvited? These are middle schoolers, after all."

The first one huffed. "Whatever, they'll work it out."

When Jesus witnessed poor treatment of a human soul, he often stepped in, sometimes defending, sometimes offending. More often, he acted with love and kindness for the oppressed. Even with known sinners, Jesus showed compassion and modeled the key premise of the Bible: he came for ALL people.

Jesus loved the world, every person, regardless of where they came from or how they behaved.

We are not privy to every student's story. We cannot comprehend the depth of pain some bring with them into our schools. Many of today's young people carry great burdens. When we observe less-than-kind behavior, we must choose whether to step in or let the group figure out the problem. Regardless, we can show the same care and concern exemplified by Jesus, just by being present.

Pray Aloud

Dear Jesus, open my eyes to see my students today. Make me aware of who may need a little extra compassion and understanding. Help me model care and concern so they learn to love one another. Amen.

Live the Lesson

How can you be present in your students' lives this week? Is there one who might benefit from a kind word or interaction on the playground? Look for students and staff who might need a Christlike lunch.

Extra Credit

Read Matthew 9. List the variety of methods Jesus used for showing compassion. What assignment does he give us at the conclusion?

Sunday Preparations

Read Aloud Ephesians 6:11

Put on the full armor of God, so that you can take your stand against the devil's schemes.

"Mom, where are my pants?"

"I need poster board!"

"I can't find my calculator."

In our house, Sunday nights equaled commotion and chaos. After a final check on lesson plans and homework, we packed lunches, reviewed the calendar, and picked clothes for the week, which at times proved to be the most difficult task. Selecting outfits required clean laundry—folded and put away—and with girls, the addition of accessories.

God deems our wardrobe important as well. In fact, he prescribes one for us. Fully aware of the enemy's schemes, God instructs his people to prepare for battle with the appropriate gear detailed in Ephesians 6. Each piece provides a specific mode of protection. From the helmet of salvation on our heads to our feet shod in the gospel, he outfits us to deter the attacks of the enemy.

Once dressed, we're instructed to take up the sword of the Spirit, the Word of God. Just as Jesus used Scripture when he faced the devil, this weapon becomes our accessory against his tactics. When tempted to judge or grow impatient, we recall to "[bear] with one another in love" (Ephesians 4:2 ESV). When offended or insulted, we remember to "forgive one another, as God in Christ forgave you" (Ephesians 4:32 ESV).

When our Sunday preparations include the full combat attire, complete with biblical armament, we are ready, with God's help, to face the week and its challenges.

Pray Aloud

Mighty Lord, without you and your Word, I am vulnerable and unable to stand against the forces of evil. I thank you for your truth and the protection you provide. Prepare me with all I need to face each day. Amen.

Live the Lesson

Consider the issues you face at school. Which part of God's armor will best protect you and your students from those attacks? Start each day dressed for success and protection.

Extra Credit

Read Ephesians 6:10–20. Inventory the garments and their purposes. Which ones are you lacking?

When We Blow It

Read Aloud 1 John 1:9

If we confess our sins, he is faithful and just and will forgive us our sins and purify us from all unrighteousness.

Kylie, a first-year special education teacher, had become a familiar face in the school. When she entered a classroom, her students left with her quietly so as not to disturb the classroom teacher.

On one occasion, the fire alarm rang ten minutes into a speech therapy session. Chaos ensued as the classroom teacher searched for the "missing" child who had departed with Kylie without his knowledge.

After the "all clear," the red-faced classroom teacher found Kylie and spewed, "Never take a child out of my room without telling me!"

Kylie apologized profusely and added, "I was sure you saw me take your student." Although Kylie never intended to cause such a ruckus, she knew she was responsible for the panic that followed. Her coworker's cutting words stayed with her all day.

As sinful people living and working in an imperfect world, we are never going to do this work perfectly. Some days, we will mess up. When our foibles directly affect others, especially our students, the sting can linger. We are wise to admit our mistakes and confess our sins.

Yet how do we move past the sharp words from others and the self-condemnation that follows? Once we confess, we must remember: Christ holds no judgment over us. His death on the cross removes all guilt and shame. Although consequences may linger, we can learn from our actions and extend grace toward ourselves, knowing we all blow it from time to time.

Kylie eventually moved on from the fateful fire drill day. Afterward, she never removed a child without first making eye contact with the classroom instructor.

Pray Aloud
Lord, I cannot accomplish anything without your guidance. Help me forgive others when they let me down and seek forgiveness when I'm the one who errs. Amen.

Live the Lesson
Do you need to confess to a coworker? Do you need to forgive yourself for an error? Search your heart and admit all sin to God. Then make things right with anyone else.

Extra Credit
Read 1 John 1–2. Look for lessons regarding sin, confession, and forgiveness through Jesus.

Spring Term

"All your movements and activities (work, school, ministry, relationships) bear witness to the power of God at work in you."

—Priscilla Shirer, *The Armor of God*

The Power of a Picture

Read Aloud 1 Peter 3:15

But in your hearts revere Christ as Lord. Always be prepared to give an answer to everyone who asks you to give the reason for the hope that you have. But do this with gentleness and respect.

When I first met Sam and his family, they spoke only Chinese. Teaching Sam English became my top educational priority. Over time, I also learned they did not know anything about Jesus, and my prayers for them intensified.

One morning, Sam's mother held one of his projects and asked, "What this shape mean?" On the painting, a white cross gleamed amid a deep purple background. She pointed to the cross shapes around the room and shrugged her shoulders. Sam's mom had no idea what the symbol represented. With joy, and as few words as possible, I explained the truth of Christ's death, his resurrection, and the meaning of the cross.

Jesus often used word pictures to help us understand difficult concepts. He compared the kingdom of heaven to a mustard seed, a pearl, a treasure, and more. Jesus drew a line in the sand to make a point about condemnation and sin. Later, the fish symbol became the secret sign of faithful followers during first-century persecution. Parables and images become effective witnessing tools when words alone cannot convey the message.

We never know what doors the Lord might open for us to witness. Even amid communication challenges, his Spirit is at work. Be ready, with whatever means he provides, to share the joy and hope we have in Christ.

Many conversations later, I offered to buy Sam's mom a Chinese Bible.

"Oh, no!" she responded. "My husband say we no believe. That Jesus be just nice man."

My prayers continued for Sam and his family to understand the true picture of Jesus.

Pray Aloud

Dear Lord, make a way for me to be a witness today. Let me not miss one opportunity to share your love with others. Even now, prepare their hearts and ears to know your truth. Amen.

Live the Lesson

Commit to praying for your students and their families to come to faith in Jesus. Then watch for opportunities to share Christ's love and message of salvation.

Extra Credit

Read John 14:15–18, 25–27. How does Jesus promise to help us with our witness?

Fighting Insecurity

Read Aloud Ephesians 3:20–21

Now to him who is able to do immeasurably more than all we ask or imagine, according to his power that is at work within us, to him be glory in the church and in Christ Jesus throughout all generations, for ever and ever! Amen.

As a student teacher in a parochial school, I was required to participate in at least one church activity outside the classroom. My supervising teacher suggested I serve as lector on a Sunday morning. When my turn came, I approached the podium with knocking knees. My hands gripped the dark wood to keep from shaking. The words swam on the page before me. When someone coughed from the congregation, I forced myself to focus on the day's Scripture reading. "From John, chapter three," I choked. After that I remember nothing, except my vow to never serve as lector in church again.

My supervisor obviously believed I was ready to read before a full church. After all, I had no trouble addressing a classroom of students. Yet after my Sunday experience, I questioned my readiness to teach as graduation loomed.

No one felt more inadequate than the apostle Paul. In his letters, he often harkened back to his days as a persecutor of Christians and expressed deep insecurity as a result. But Paul learned over time that his readiness depended not on his history or skills but on Christ's power at work in him.

We, too, can teach and work in our classrooms with confidence, not relying solely on our own abilities but trusting in Jesus to equip and empower us. Of course we need teaching strategies and experience to hone those skills, but with his power, God elevates our efforts.

When we invite Jesus into each lesson, reading, or lecture, our insecurities fade, God fills in our gaps, and we give him all the glory.

Pray Aloud
Holy Lord, equip me today! Remove any insecurities and empower me with your Holy Spirit so that I can accomplish all that you have for me in this classroom. Amen.

Live the Lesson
Which of your students exhibit insecurities, especially when called upon to read or recite aloud? How could you encourage them and help them grow in confidence?

Extra Credit
Read Ephesians 3. Mine these verses for the nuggets of truth regarding our Source of power and strength.

School Unity

Read Aloud Ephesians 4:3

Make every effort to keep the unity of the Spirit through the bond of peace.

Seeing a note on her desk didn't surprise Meghan. Her students or their parents often left messages at the end of the day. But the contents of this one made her gasp.

"I am so sorry," it read. "I'm dealing with a lot at home, and the stress followed me to school, making me cranky with students and coworkers." Meghan lowered the note and reflected on the tension she and this colleague had experienced in recent weeks. *I thought it was me.* Immediately, Meghan sought out the friend to assure her and to pray with her.

Have you noticed how the challenges of life manage to worm their way into our work? We become short-tempered, irritable, and, sometimes, irrational. We think, *I must have done something wrong.* Satan takes advantage of our pressures and weasels his way into our day, tempting us to lash out at those we love and serve. He disrupts our peace and damages our relationships.

How do we combat the issue? Meghan and her coworker modeled several important methods. The first involved communication and confession. The simple note of apology and explanation dissolved the tension between the friends like hot water over ice. The alternative—refusing to share any personal problems—can lead to miscommunication, hurt feelings, and, sometimes, the end of a friendship. The coworker didn't divulge any details, yet her tidbit of transparency and confession went a long way to rebuilding trust.

Meghan demonstrated our second lesson. Not only did she quickly forgive but intentionally did so face-to-face, followed by an offer to pray with her friend. When we unite before Jesus, the enemy becomes powerless to establish a foothold in our relationships.

Do you want peace in your classroom, in your school? Make every attempt to communicate, forgive, and pray. These efforts exemplify the unity of the Spirit, which leads to peace.

Pray Aloud
Dear Lord, we need your Holy Spirit's power to conquer the enemy's divisive tactics. Unite our hearts and make us bold to communicate love and forgiveness to one another. Amen.

Live the Lesson
With whom do you need to make peace? Commit to rectifying the situation this week. The sacrifice of pride and privacy is worth unity and victory.

Extra Credit
Read Ephesians 4:17–32. Study the guidelines for living and working with others.

Swarming

Read Aloud Mark 15:9-11

"Do you want me to release to you the king of the Jews?" asked Pilate, knowing it was out of self-interest that the chief priests had handed Jesus over to him. But the chief priests stirred up the crowd to have Pilate release Barabbas instead.

The principal stared at his computer screen in shock. The negative statements he read on the school's parent forum made him shake his head in disbelief.

"This is ridiculous!" wrote one angry parent. "The administration needs to do something!"

"It's that teacher. He has it out for my son," another replied.

"We're ready to pull our kids. Who's with me?" wrote another.

He shut off the comments on the post and sighed. *When did these parents turn against the school? Last week they praised us.* Somehow one playground incident triggered buzzing like a bear to a bee's nest.

A similar surge occurred during the time we now refer to as Holy Week. The celebratory atmosphere of Christ's welcoming procession into Jerusalem quickly turned to questioning, criticizing, and condemnation. Only four days separated the "Hosanna" cheers from the "Crucify him!" chants. God permitted the human mob tendency to accomplish his plan of salvation, namely, the suffering and death of Jesus on the cross.

Today's swarming, although not always violent in nature, works as the name suggests. Energized individuals increase in number and, at times, ferocity. Like bees on a mission, some folks relish in provoking others toward their cause.

Most beekeepers take a gentle approach to swarms, scooping small groups of bees and coaxing them to their hive. Having the queen present attracts the others to settle in. I believe handling bees takes the patience and courage of Christ. Likewise, our approach to angry parents requires the grace and wisdom of Jesus to handle with care.

Pray Aloud
Dear Jesus, I am grateful for your work on the cross. Forgive me for when I follow the crowd or become drawn into arguments. Help me show grace and forgiveness in all situations. Amen.

Live the Lesson
What is your typical response to mob behavior in the workplace? Search in Scripture for the methods Christ used to defuse negativity.

Extra Credit
Read James 1:19–27. Search for God-pleasing responses to anger.

Fifty-Six More Days

Read Aloud Hebrews 12:2 (BSB)
Let us fix our eyes on Jesus, the author and perfecter of our faith, who for the joy set before Him endured the cross, scorning its shame, and sat down at the right hand of the throne of God.

With a sigh, I shut down my work computer. "March lesson plans done!" I said to my empty classroom. *Only three more months until summer break.* Although passionate about teaching, I also love the warm summer months. On this occasion, during a particularly difficult year, I found myself counting the days. A challenging class, plus difficult parents, combined with personal struggles induced a longing for the rest and restart summer would bring.

However, when we focus on the future, we may miss the blessings in front of us. When we fix our eyes on what's to come, even needed rest and vacation, we may miss opportunities to influence our students in the time we have left. The clock may be dragging for us, but time is also running out on our days to impact our current class. Now is the time to nurture, teach, and influence our students.

If we fix our eyes anywhere, let us fix them on Jesus. Acquainted with a time line and facing difficult tasks, he endured much more than a few months of school. Indeed, he endured the suffering for the joy that would follow. His faithfulness to his calling motivates us to follow suit.

What if we altered the fifty-six-more-days mindset to *only* fifty-six more days *left* to make a difference? With Christ's strength and example, we can persist to the end and finally delight in the respite to follow.

Pray Aloud
Jesus, help me stay focused on you today. Keep my mind on the tasks before me and show me how you continue to accomplish your good work. Give me the energy to stay the course. Amen.

Live the Lesson
If you want to count the days, go ahead. Then post the number somewhere with the word *only* attached. Embrace the old saying, "Rather than count the days, make each day count."

Extra Credit
Read Psalm 90. Search for God's concept of time.

The Workers Are Few

Read Aloud Luke 10:2

He told them, "The harvest is plentiful, but the workers are few. Ask the Lord of the harvest, therefore, to send out workers in his harvest field."

Seven months into the school year, a young teacher phoned his parents.

"I just can't keep doing this," he told them. "I've tried. My principal has offered to give me a different grade next fall, but I'm not sure it would help."

His mom and dad heard the agony in their son's voice and began to pray even before he finished sharing.

For many new teachers, a career in the classroom has proved more challenging than they anticipated. After four years of higher education, including student teaching, some experience crushing disappointment when they discover a growing lack of parental involvement or weak administrative support. Occasionally, teachers discover they were not properly prepared for the hostility and disrespect they receive from some of their students. As teachers leave the profession due to these and other causes, the need for teachers—well-trained and prepared for the current climate and culture—continues to rise.

However, our current circumstances do not surprise our Lord. He is aware of the happenings in today's classrooms. He is working at this moment to prepare the next generation to accomplish his will in our schools and with our future children. He instructs us to ask him to meet this need. His request in Luke 10:2 means he welcomes our involvement in his plan for our world, including our schools. By involving us, we have the privilege to participate and recognize his faithfulness when he answers our prayers.

As our educational teams work to encourage and support new teachers, we can trust our Lord to continue to provide more leaders in the classroom. We need only ask.

Pray Aloud

Lord, you see the need for more equipped and dedicated educators. Please raise up new leaders to nurture the next generation. Show me how I can encourage those around me to stay the course. Amen.

Live the Lesson

Does your school have enough teachers for the coming school year? If not, gather in the vacant classrooms and ask the Lord to meet those needs. Thank him in advance for the person he already has in mind.

Extra Credit

Read Luke 10. Identify Jesus's methods for sending his workers. In what ways did his followers in this chapter live and witness?

Wardrobe Malfunction

Read Aloud Ephesians 4:22-24

You were taught, with regard to your former way of life, to put off your old self, which is being corrupted by its deceitful desires; to be made new in the attitude of your minds; and to put on the new self, created to be like God in true righteousness and holiness.

The high school drama department was in full swing. With the premier only a week away, rehearsals continued amid pit practices and set construction. Costumes for this production proved extra challenging as the lead female character required more costume changes than a Taylor Swift concert.

Opening night, although an overall success, yielded a few glitches: an audience member's phone rang and an unplanned cymbal clanged backstage. In the finale, the female lead entered wearing a sparkling white wedding gown—with the black skirt from the previous scene trailing behind her.

From preschool dress-up to college productions, people enjoy donning costumes and assuming different roles. The very young imagine their future occupation. Older thespians relish the opportunity to portray a life not their own, if only on a stage.

In Christ, we obtain a new existence. No longer cloaked in darkness and consumed by sin, believers receive a new life in Jesus. His work on the cross replaces our sin-stained apparel and provides us with a fresh wardrobe—clean and white—to present us holy and righteous before the Father.

Yet occasionally, our words and actions expose our old selves and allow our sin nature to peek out under our new attire: we snap at a student or are drawn into gossip. We judge a parent or show disrespect. Even as Christians, we cannot conceal our sinfulness entirely this side of heaven. When we let the old self show, repentance must follow. Then we can receive Jesus's forgiveness and wear white again with joy.

Pray Aloud

Jesus, forgive me for the times I fall and fail in my Christian walk. Thank you for your mercy and grace. Amen.

Live the Lesson

Have you let your sinful nature peek out under your Christlike cloak? Repent and receive forgiveness, allowing the new garments to outshine the old.

Extra Credit

Read Romans 6. Study how Christ's death and resurrection transform our spiritual wardrobe.

Show the Glow

Read Aloud 1 Peter 2:9 (ESV)
But you are a chosen race, a royal priesthood, a holy nation, a people for his own possession, that you may proclaim the excellencies of him who called you out of darkness into his marvelous light.

Outdoor gym class began as usual. Two self-appointed captains quickly divided the students, forming softball teams. First to be chosen were the top hitters and next the mediocre players, leaving the less-than-athletic group destined for the outfield.

Except on this day, one captain looked sharply at his final choice, a lanky-legged blonde girl whose red face stared at the dirt. When he called her name and directed her to second base, both teams gasped. One classmate threw down his mitt and cried, "We've already lost!"

The girl didn't care. The size of her smile rivaled the distance to home plate. Her face reflected the joy in her heart because she had been chosen.

Do you remember that we, too, were chosen?

If we have known Christ all our lives, have been brought up in the church, and cannot remember *not* being his, we can forget our adoption into his priesthood of believers. We neglect to recall our rescue and take for granted the truth that we've been handpicked. And it shows.

The struggles in this life distract us. Our trials drag us down until our faces resemble forgotten outfielders rather than beloved children of God. Will you do yourself a favor today and remind your face? Wear the joy of being a member of the royal family.

A dozen dropped balls later and a wide-margin loss couldn't erase the glow from the girl's countenance. Let's do likewise and show the glow. Our King, *the* King, chose us.

Pray Aloud

Jesus, thank you for choosing me. Thank you for rescuing me from sin and making me your child. Let your light shine brightly through me so that others may see your reflection. Amen.

Live the Lesson

Ponder the reality of your priesthood. Challenge yourself to smile more today. When your students ask you about your grin, tell them, "We're royalty."

Extra Credit

Read Psalm 98. Relish in the joy of the Lord.

The Great Protector

Read Aloud Matthew 23:37
Jerusalem, Jerusalem, you who kill the prophets and stone those sent to you, how often I have longed to gather your children together, as a hen gathers her chicks under her wings, and you were not willing.

A bright flash accompanied the simultaneous *Crack . . . Boom!*, bringing darkness to the classroom. Some children screamed while others whimpered, until the teacher's soothing voice drew them to her comforting presence. "Come toward me!" she called. Never had she felt such a strong sense of protection. She knelt and spread her arms wide, attempting to encompass the large group of frightened students. Only a few stood aloof with nervous chuckles, wanting to be near without admitting to it.

Like these too-cool students, we sometimes resist the comfort of our Great Protector. The self-sufficient declare, "I can handle this!" The proud pronounce, "I don't need him." The sinner says, "He doesn't want me."

Yet if you look carefully at today's verse, Christ's love was not contingent upon the condition of the subject. He called out their sin but continued with his longing to comfort them and his grief at their resistance.

Jesus says the same to us. He knows all about our pride and sin. He is aware of any anger or regret we may be feeling. His work on the cross already took care of those hindrances that keep us from running to him. He loves us and longs to draw us into his protective embrace. Today's verse demonstrates his grief when we refuse him. Whether this life brings us storms or fair weather, the Lord Jesus invites us into his comforting arms. Will you come?

Pray Aloud
Dear God, when trouble arises, help me remember I am not alone. I can call out to you and run into your arms for safety and assurance. Amen.

Live the Lesson
When have you resisted looking to Jesus for protection or comfort? What stood in the way? He can handle all our feelings, including any anger, fear, or self-sufficiency.

Extra Credit
Read Psalm 46. How does this chapter bring you comfort?

A Steady Race

Read Aloud Hebrews 12:1

Therefore, since we are surrounded by such a great cloud of witnesses, let us throw off everything that hinders and the sin that so easily entangles. And let us run with perseverance the race marked out for us.

Red-faced runners pushed ahead with arms and elbows shoving, legs and hips angling to be first. The winner broke past the pack, all smiles. The losers collapsed, some in tears. You'd have thought it was the race of a lifetime.

"Straight line!" the teacher called. Recess was over.

For some kids, attaining front-line status equals winning the Olympics. Even at recess, kids run as if their lives depend on it.

As teachers, we do, too, with long days in the classroom followed by longer nights marking papers, entering grades, and responding to parents. Does our life or classroom success truly rely on how hard we push ourselves?

Our verse encourages us to run with perseverance and tenacity, even when the effort becomes difficult. Yet this description sounds more like a long-distance race than a sprint. Short-distance competitors run fast and hard like our recess racers. Cross-country runners understand the length of the course. They expect and watch for markers indicating twists and turns and uphill challenges. So they pace themselves and sprint only when necessary.

God has marked our path. He encourages us to keep on, but he doesn't expect us to run at full speed all the time. No one can keep that up. He urges us to persist, but at a steady rate.

When we feel our strength waning and are ready to drop, it's time to slow the pace, find refreshment, and even stop for a while if needed. Rest assured, the finish line is just ahead. With God's help, we can stay the course and finish the race.

Pray Aloud
Lord God, when work feels like an uphill race, strengthen me. When I feel off course, steady me. Lead and guide my steps as I follow you. Amen.

Live the Lesson
This week, stop running for a minute. Try walking instead. Then, at the next opportunity, find time to rest. Look around and see how far you've come.

Extra Credit
Read Isaiah 40. Savor the promises within.

There's a Snake in Our School!

Read Aloud 2 Corinthians 11:3

But I am afraid that just as Eve was deceived by the serpent's cunning, your minds may somehow be led astray from your sincere and pure devotion to Christ.

What began as a day worth celebrating turned dreadful with a startling sight. The warm sunshine welcomed my class outdoors, where the students could finally run around without coats. While the children lined up, I stepped into my storage area to grab a few playground toys. A swift slithering movement in the corner of the closet made me jump back and scream, startling the children. Their cacophony of shrieks caught the attention of the custodian.

"Thank goodness you're here," I said above the din. "There's a snake in the school!"

The children and I observed the custodian capture and release the intruder into a nearby field. *What would prevent the creature from creeping back in?* I wondered.

Indeed, a snake does attempt to inhabit our schools. Not the innocent garter snake that shows itself after a long winter's nap, but a deceiver who brings chaos to the classroom, sows division among our staff, and attempts to thwart our efforts to teach truth and walk in the light of Christ. Look around. He shows up everywhere: in the halls among gossiping students, in staff meetings amid disagreements, and online when parents complain and slander. The snake sneaks into our schools to divide and destroy.

We don't have to face this serpent alone. Like the available custodian, Jesus—when invited into our situations—contends with the deceiver for us. Cry out to him, not with shrieks of fear but with confidence in prayer. Resist the enemy's attempts to create chaos by calling on Christ's name. He who defeated this foe through his death on the cross stands ready to exterminate our enemy again.

Pray Aloud

Jesus, we pray against Satan's work and ask for your protection from his divisive and deceiving ways. Keep our hearts and minds focused on you so that we cannot be led astray. Amen.

Live the Lesson

Where do you see the enemy at work in your school? Take those matters to Christ in prayer. Ask God to fight these battles and rid your school of gossip, slander, and division.

Extra Credit

Read 1 Peter 5:1–11. What warnings are given in these verses? What assurances are offered?

Mary Had a Little Goat

Read Aloud Romans 8:1

Therefore, there is now no condemnation for those who are in Christ Jesus.

What started as an innocent show-and-tell event turned into chaos when a visiting goat shared more than expected. As the droppings rolled in all directions, my students roared with laughter and backstepped in unison like a well-choreographed dance. I grabbed a broom and frantically brushed the marble-shaped contents off the slick floor into a dustpan until I heard my principal's voice.

"What in the world?!"

His tone persuaded me to forgo my task and explain. Red-faced, I rose and glanced at the handler who now cradled the goat in her arms. "I . . . she . . ." I took a breath. "I was told they visit nursing homes. It's perfectly safe."

"But not sanitary," he said through his teeth. "Take the goat out. And next time, keep live animals outside!"

I chuckle at the memory now, but at the time, the mortification and embarrassment stayed with me all day. My principal had every reason to scold. I had made a mistake and earned his reprimand.

We deserve God's condemnation as well when we daily fall short of the Father's expectations. Thanks be to God for his forgiving grace given to us by Christ's death and resurrection. God's love is not contingent upon our efforts or attempts to earn his favor. He offers full forgiveness, sweeping up our past and removing our sins forever.

Our students make mistakes as well. Whether done willfully or carelessly, their frustrating behavior can irritate and even infuriate us, especially the repeat offenders. More than classroom management strategies, teachers require God-sized patience. Just as God willingly forgives and forgets our sins, he provides all we need to address and pardon our students.

My principal never mentioned the goat incident again, and my students met all four-legged visitors outside on the grass from then on.

Pray Aloud
Gracious Lord, thank you for your sacrifice on the cross and the gift of forgiveness. Fill me with love for my students and the patience to model your mercy and grace. Amen.

Live the Lesson
Which of your students requires the most effort and patience? Thank God for them and commit to praying for them daily.

Extra Credit
Read Matthew 18. What lessons on sin, forgiveness, and relationships do we receive from this chapter?

A Final Blessing

Read Aloud Numbers 6:23-27

"Tell Aaron and his sons, 'This is how you are to bless the Israelites. Say to them:

> *"'"The Lord bless you*
> *and keep you;*
> *the Lord make his face shine on you*
> *and be gracious to you;*
> *the Lord turn his face toward you*
> *and give you peace."'*

"So they will put my name on the Israelites, and I will bless them."

"The Lord bless and keep you," the teachers sang over their students.

"May his face shine upon you," the children responded.

"May he always be with you," the group sang in unison. "And give you peace." The voices faded at the conclusion of the closing chapel service.

The principal looked over the sea of heads and took note of those who would not return in the fall. Some students would graduate, others would move. A couple needed more help than this school could offer. The latter brought tears to her eyes. *What will they do? Who will help them?*

Saying goodbye to our students at the end of the year can bring a mixture of joy and sadness. While some have been challenging, others brought us daily joy. After we have poured love and effort into each one, and faithfully prayed for them, our hearts ache knowing we may never set eyes on some hereafter.

The familiar words from Numbers had one purpose: to bless the Israelites as they departed. The Lord instructed Aaron and his sons to put the name of God on them as we see in the verse following the benediction. By doing so, God applied his own name, identifying the people as his precious possession.

Likewise, we do not send our students off alone. With God's blessing upon them, his gifts of grace, favor, and peace accompany them. The children depart with the Holy God who claims them as his own.

Pray Aloud

Heavenly Father, go with my students this summer and into the next season of their lives. For those who will not return to us, we pray a special blessing. Let them never forget your love. Amen.

Live the Lesson

Are there students you are concerned about? Add their names to your calendar as a reminder to continue to pray for them. Trust that God goes with them.

Extra Credit

Read Numbers 6:22–27 and Isaiah 49. Reflect on God's love for his children.

Summer Term

The Lord is my shepherd; I shall not want.
  He makes me lie down in green pastures.
He leads me beside still waters.
  He restores my soul.

—Psalm 23:1–3 (ESV)

Used Up

Read Aloud 1 Kings 19:3-4

Elijah was afraid and ran for his life. When he came to Beersheba in Judah, he left his servant there, while he himself went a day's journey into the wilderness. He came to a broom bush, sat down under it and prayed that he might die. "I have had enough, Lord," he said. "Take my life; I am no better than my ancestors."

A kindergartner ran to his mom and wrapped his arms around her legs.

"Hi sweetie," his mom said, returning the hug. She made eye contact with his teacher and asked her son, "Did you have a good day?" The teacher's nod brought a sigh of relief.

Once in the car, however, the boy's mood shifted, first with a soulful plea to stop at the park, followed by a tantrum at her firm no.

The mother ignored her son's tears until their van pulled into the driveway. She waited until he quieted before asking, "You behaved in class today. Why are you acting like this now?"

The boy thought for moment then replied, "I guess I used up all my good at school."

Today's verse speaks of Elijah, a prophet of God, who ran to the wilderness, his body, mind, and soul spent. To understand his plight, we must look back at the events preceding his exhaustion. In 1 Kings 17 and 18, we witness God's might as he fed Elijah by way of ravens, provided unending oil and flour for a widow, and to top it all off, raised the same widow's son from the dead. Then, Elijah faced four hundred fifty false prophets in the sacrificial showdown of a lifetime.

After participating in these miracles, Elijah wanted to quit and begged the Lord to take his life. We wonder at Elijah's fear and despondency after such a remarkable display of God's power until we remember that the great prophet was merely human, just like we are.

Like Elijah, our patience, strength, and stamina eventually wane. No one can continue to pour into others without periods of rest and rejuvenation. The Lord met Elijah in his exhausted state and met his needs. He will do the same for us.

Our tired boy required a nap after his work at school. Perhaps we do too.

Pray Aloud
Heavenly Father, during this summer break, give my body, soul, and spirit rest. Restore my energy and sharpen my mind so that I can continue to serve you. Amen.

Live the Lesson
We know the old saying, "You can't pour from an empty cup." Relax and be nourished with activities that restore and refresh.

Extra Credit
Read Psalm 23. Savor the words and heed the invitation to rest in the Shepherd's arms.

Joy Lost and Found

Read Aloud Romans 14:17

For the kingdom of God is not a matter of eating and drinking, but of righteousness, peace and joy in the Holy Spirit.

"I need to see you in my office."

The principal's words filled the teacher with dread. As she followed her administrator down the hall, a list of possible topics rolled through her mind. *Did I do something wrong? Is it an angry parent? Bad news from home?* She took a deep breath and sat across from his desk.

He paused before speaking, folding his hands as if in prayer. "I'm concerned about you," he said at last. "You've lost your joy."

She felt heat rise to her hairline. "I don't understand," she whispered.

"You arrived here last fall with such joy and enthusiasm in the Lord and for your work," he explained. "What's happened?"

Indeed, what transforms a joy-filled servant, eager to serve her students and instruct with confidence, into one so despondent that friends and colleagues take notice? Difficult students, frustrating coworkers, circumstances outside the classroom—the list is endless of the potential situations that threaten to bring us down.

Our joy does not depend on our external issues but on peace and confidence in Christ. When we take our eyes off Jesus and fixate on the problems around us, our joy wanes. Our peace dissipates. And it shows.

For this teacher, the transition came slowly, first, with the difficulty of adjusting to new surroundings. She underestimated the stress of a new job in a new place. Second, she had befriended a crabby neighbor with whom to share God's love. However, the reverse occurred as the negativity affected the vulnerable teacher. She explained all this to her concerned principal who listened patiently.

"You know where and from Whom our joy comes," he gently reminded her.

She nodded. Together they prayed for renewed joy and peace.

Pray Aloud
Father, when I take my eyes off you, I focus on the troubles around me and flounder. Remind me of your great love. Fill me with your peace. And let my joy be evident to all as a testimony of your faithfulness. Amen.

Live the Lesson
On a scale of 1 to 10, how would you rate your level of joy? Are you focused on circumstances or on Christ? Thank God for ten blessings right now.

Extra Credit
Read Romans 14. What various thoughts and attitudes interfere with our joy in Christ?

Uprooted

Read Aloud Matthew 16:24

Then Jesus said to his disciples, "Whoever wants to be my disciple must deny themselves and take up their cross and follow me."

The tears flowed unchecked as I boxed the last of my teaching supplies. Once again, I prepared to say goodbye to teachers and families I had served and grown to love. This was not the first time I packed up a classroom, and I presumed it would not be the last. After seven relocations, I concluded that no teaching assignment lasts forever.

Jesus's words—*follow me*—imply a journey with movement and motion. Rarely staying in one place, Jesus exemplified our temporary residence on this earth and considered heaven our final destination. Our call to teach has less to do with where we serve and more to do with following where Christ leads. Although not always obvious, this calling exemplifies God's desire to include us in his plan, that all will know him and be saved (1 Timothy 2:4).

Perhaps you've had the joy of serving in the same location your entire career. I confess I envy those who have had that privilege. These truths are for you as well. God weaves your current and future call into his greater plans. One day he may say, "Follow me into a new career" or "Follow me into retirement." Either way, you do not travel alone or without purpose.

Indeed, our journey with Jesus keeps us on the move. Though painful to pack up and pick up, we can follow in faith, trusting in God's guidance and promise of his presence.

Pray Aloud

Lord, I recognize this is your assignment for me right now. Thank you for the honor of being used by you and making me part of your bigger plan. Help me shine brightly here until you call me away. Amen.

Live the Lesson

Are you content where you are right now, or are you feeling restless? Thank God for your current position and trust him to lead if a transition is in your future.

Extra Credit

Read Matthew 16. Note the challenges Jesus faced in this chapter. How does this apply to following him?

"I Can" Statement

Read Aloud Philippians 4:12-13

I know what it is to be in need, and I know what it is to have plenty. I have learned the secret of being content in any and every situation, whether well fed or hungry, whether living in plenty or in want. I can do all this through him who gives me strength.

The teacher stared at the official-looking letter, trying to take in its contents. The subpoena involved a custody battle over a current student. She had already shared reams of documentation and participated in multiple interviews with the child's guardian ad litem. She had hoped her responsibilities to this troubled family would be completed once the school year ended. But now . . . *this*. Her heart pounded as she realized what the notice conveyed: the unfolding drama would extend far into the summer and into a courtroom.

Our struggles exist inside and outside of the classroom. The challenges come home with us, follow us into our dreams, and occasionally go beyond the borders of the school year—the sum of which drains our reserves, leaving us parched in soul and spirit.

Like a cup of cold water, Paul's familiar words in Philippians bring relief to a thirsty soul. First, he shares the challenges he has faced, followed by an "I can" declaration disclosing his method for obtaining peace despite his circumstances. That he penned this letter from prison emphasizes his point. Paul found contentment, even while under house arrest, by leaning on the One who never tires.

When school difficulties push beyond the classroom walls and school calendar, we need not face them alone. As Paul implies, we can do anything, face any challenge, accomplish any task, but not on our own. We can with the help and strength of Christ.

Pray Aloud
God of the Universe, you are all-knowing and all-seeing. You know every need. Provide the energy and courage for the challenges ahead. Amen.

Live the Lesson
What big challenge do you face now? Create an "I Can" statement with Jesus as your source of strength.

Extra Credit
Read Philippians 4. What commands are stated in verses 4–6? Look to verse 7 for the result. Add these truths to your "I Can" statement.

Independence

Read Aloud Psalm 62:5-7 (GNT)
I depend on God alone;
 I put my hope in him.
He alone protects and saves me;
 he is my defender,
 and I shall never be defeated.
My salvation and honor depend on God;
 he is my strong protector;
 he is my shelter.

In mid-spring, a daycare director contacted me to substitute in July. "I need to set this up early," she told me. "The teacher of the two-year-olds has asked for an extended visit to her homeland."

"Two weeks of summer with twos?" I asked. Having worked with this age group before, I agreed, but knew I'd have my hands full. Regular diaper changes, meals without silverware, and plenty of "Me do it!" would fill my days. Yet despite the familiar terrible-two reputation, I looked forward to the children's delightfully developing language and fierce fight toward independence.

Unfortunately, two weeks turned into three weeks and then into four. For an unexplained reason, the foreign government detained the teacher, delaying her return to her home in the United States, her family, and her students. While she fought for freedom, I wrestled with toddlers battling for their own independence.

As Americans, we appreciate the struggle for autonomy. We celebrate our independence each year, as we should—that is, unless our fight for freedom includes independence from our Creator. At times, we neglect prayer and ignore reading our Bibles, determined to live life on our own. Like my toddler friends, we declare "Me do it!" As a result, we deny the aid of the One who helps us through the most exhausting days. He alone strengthens and saves us. For if we reject God's monarchy, we reject him and his plan for our lives. Instead, let's celebrate our *dependence* on the Lord who reigns on high.

By summer's end, many of the two-year-olds could put their own bedding away, and some even conquered potty training. Eventually the teacher returned, and I enjoyed my own liberation from the terrific twos.

Pray Aloud

Father, you are my fortress and my protector. When I am tempted to tackle life without you, remind me of the hope and strength found only in you. Amen.

Live the Lesson

In what ways do you depend on God? How do you lean on him for all your needs? Make prayer and Bible reading a daily activity.

Extra Credit

Read Psalms 62 and 63. How did David lean on God?

A Time for Everything

Read Aloud Ecclesiastes 3:1-6

There is a time for everything,
 and a season for every activity under the heavens:

a time to be born and a time to die,
a time to plant and a time to uproot,
a time to kill and a time to heal,
a time to tear down and a time to build,
a time to weep and a time to laugh,
a time to mourn and a time to dance,
a time to scatter stones and a time to gather them
a time to embrace and a time to refrain from embracing,
a time to search and a time to give up,
a time to keep and a time to throw away.

As my son and I approached the scout meeting, we could hear the noise through the walls. He immediately zoomed past me to join the fray. Once in the door, I dodged boys in blue uniforms darting about and searched for familiar faces. After spotting my friends, I sat down and closed my eyes, hoping to shut out the din, reciting the mantra: *The mayhem is not my problem; teacher hat off, mom hat on.* After a peek at my watch, my gaze shifted to the front of the room. The men in tan uniforms, seemingly oblivious to the chaos, would soon call the meeting to order.

Many people thrive and even welcome commotion. Take these scouts, for instance. At their young age, movement and noise were as natural to them as to the bear cubs on their patches. Stillness and order required more resources than they possessed. Someday they would learn the importance of sitting and listening.

The verses in Ecclesiastes portray this balance with multiple scenarios. Activities that evoke disorder, such as uprooting, tearing down, and scattering stones feel messy and produce uneasiness. Most prefer life to death, healing to killing, and building to destroying. For those who prefer calm over crazy, remember that destruction must precede for the building to occur. Indeed, the weeding comes before planting, and the planting before harvesting.

Later, my son, his troop, and several of us moms enjoyed the results of those wild meetings when we attended summer camp together. There the boys climbed and tumbled through the days until their tired bodies collapsed in cots, refueling for the next day.

Pray Aloud

Lord, thank you for pursuits that work our bodies and nurture our minds. Thank you for peaceful moments and rest. Amen.

Live the Lesson

What needs uprooting from your life, house, or classroom? Clear the clutter and search for ways to find balance as you approach the school year.

Extra Credit

Read Ecclesiastes 3. What is God revealing to you through these words?

Donut Encounter

Read Aloud John 4:13-14

Jesus answered, "Everyone who drinks this water will be thirsty again, but whoever drinks the water I give them will never thirst. Indeed, the water I give them will become in them a spring of water welling up to eternal life."

The bell rang, dismissing the summer band camp. As students packed up their instruments, the teacher called one teen over to the piano. The junior from the brass section had refused to audition for the men's choir despite the teacher's best efforts. Today, he was ready with a new tactic. "I'll give you this donut if you sing a few notes for me," he challenged the tall, lanky boy. "Let's hear how low you can go."

The student eyed the treat, its sugary scent and chocolate glaze causing his stomach to rumble. After a quick scan of the now-empty room, the teenager said, "Yeah, I'll try. Guess I need a snack."

When Jesus met the Samaritan woman at Jacob's well, he understood her exact needs. She went to the well to quench her thirst; Jesus suggested *living water*. She planned to fill jugs for cooking and cleaning; he intended to cleanse her of her sin and restore her soul. Jesus arranged this encounter to offer what no one else could: a new life and eternal future with him.

The exchange with Jesus changed the woman's life. He forgave her sins and renewed her joy, setting the Samaritan on a new course. She embarked on a mission to share the transformative power of her "Messiah meeting."

After the donut challenge, the teen's life altered as well. His voice proved to be an excellent bass, prompting him to join three choirs his senior year. In college, he enrolled in the music education program. Today, he instructs youth in choir and band and initiates purposeful conversations with his students.

Never underestimate the power of divine meetings. When Christ is present, lives change, with or without donuts.

Pray Aloud
Father, provide opportunities for me to connect with my students. Be present in those conversations and use these engagements to encourage and equip the young people around me. Amen.

Live the Lesson
As you pray, listen for promptings of the Holy Spirit. Be willing and available for God-ordained appointments.

Extra Credit
Read John 4. Pay special attention to the circumstances surrounding this unusual meeting. What were the consequences?

Summer Surrender

Read Aloud Jeremiah 29:11

"For I know the plans I have for you," declares the Lord, "plans to prosper you and not to harm you, plans to give you hope and a future."

A teen fell to her knees with tears and sweat pouring down her face. Alone in the house, the girl sobbed without inhibition. The last few years had been difficult, including a move and changing schools, both preempted by a car accident that claimed the life of her mom. Many tears had preceded these, those of heartbreak, anxiety, and weeping through the "whys."

These tears, however, were different. This breakdown brought unexplained relief and joy. "God, if you care, show me. I need you," she cried. "Take it all. I surrender my life, my future. Take my sin. Forgive me for turning my back on you."

With shaky hands, she read the words on the 3x5 card again. "For I know the plans I have for you . . ." The verse had been put to memory months ago in her high school religion class. On this hot July day, the Old Testament promise hit its mark.

Jeremiah, often called the weeping prophet, penned the words of hope during a time of great grief and despair. The people had rebelled and turned from God, leading to their eventual downfall and exile to Babylon. God's words to his people through Jeremiah showed his undying love and longing to see his people repent and return to him.

The Lord continues to call all mankind to himself. The Bible conveys the way back to a restored relationship with our Creator through Jesus. His death and resurrection promise a future in which mourners are comforted and joy abounds.

God's message did not convince the kingdom of Judah in time to avoid its punishment, but the lesson reached a girl in this century and broke through her misery. Through a teacher's religion assignment, long after grades had been entered, God restored a soul to himself.

Pray Aloud

Dear Lord, young people today face many challenges. They deal with much anxiety and confusion. Bring your messages of hope to them through your Word. Amen.

Live the Lesson

Did this devotion bring someone to mind as you read it? Pray for that individual, asking God to continue to work in their life. If appropriate, reach out to express your concern and support.

Extra Credit

Read Jeremiah 29. Study the context surrounding the familiar verses we pull out of Jeremiah. Where were God's people? Why were his promises so meaningful?

Unexpected Storm

Read Aloud Psalm 61:1-2

Hear my cry, O God;
listen to my prayer.

From the ends of the earth I call to you,
I call as my heart grows faint;
lead me to the rock that is higher than I.

During a summer session, my class attended a local play. At the conclusion of the show, the students followed me to the theater's exit, where we discovered a storm had moved in during the performance. The crowds poured out of the building into the driving rain. "Stay close," I warned. En masse, we moved toward the buses. After spotting our school's number, I made a sharp right toward our ride. As soon as our drenched group settled into their seats, a count of heads revealed the worst fear: a child was missing.

After informing the other chaperones, I raced onto each bus in the line shouting, "Please don't leave! We lost a child!" Up and down the steps I repeated the same plea and asked everyone to recount and search. Eventually, the missing student, who had turned left in the crowd, was found. I hadn't realized how rapidly the unexpected storm could lead to confusion and underestimated its blinding effect on my students and me.

How true this is for us when storms of life emerge unexpectedly. We think we can manage. *It's just a little rain*, we think.

We forget how challenging circumstances can cloud our judgment and that of those around us.

David faced the storm of his life through the choices he made with Bathsheba. After years of following the Lord and remaining steadfast, he rushed headlong into a relationship that led him from one tempest to another, all at his own doing. Not until Nathan confronted the king did David finally repent.

Scholars believe David wrote many of the psalms with his adultery and reconciliation with God in mind. He trusted in the One who would deliver him from himself and his sin.

When the storms in life threaten to overtake us, we search for the Rock, our firm foundation, who lifts us above the storm to security and a clearer view.

Pray Aloud
Almighty God, I have no idea what challenges I will face today. Keep my feet planted firmly on you, my Rock and Fortress from the storm. Amen.

Live the Lesson
Can you recall a time when the storms of life blindsided you? Did you find yourself confused and making errors? Step closer to the Rock this week. Read his Word and attend worship.

Extra Credit
Read Psalm 61. How do these verses strengthen you?

Sabbath Saboteurs

Read Aloud Genesis 2:1–3

Thus the heavens and the earth were completed in all their vast array. By the seventh day God had finished the work he had been doing; so on the seventh day he rested from all his work. Then God blessed the seventh day and made it holy, because on it he rested from all the work of creating that he had done.

"Yeah! All right!" The cheering and high-fives from my boys could be heard from the dining room where I worked. I wondered if a fabulous play or actual touchdown prompted the applause. Opening a tab on my laptop, I peeked at the score. *Yes!* The Packers were back on top.

I promptly returned to the main screen and continued entering grades, longing to join the fun in the other room. There was no time to ponder how often I spent Sunday afternoons on schoolwork instead of with family. *Just finish, and maybe you can catch the fourth quarter*, I resolved.

When God designed a day of rest, he did so for our sakes, not his own. He gave the concept top priority among the commandments, "Remember the Sabbath day by keeping it holy" (Exodus 20:8). His six-day creation established our workweek followed by a break from labor to rejuvenate our bodies, minds, and souls.

Yet even when we understand this truth, activities seem to sneak into our Sunday and sabotage our Sabbath. Housework, yard maintenance, and homework demand our attention and compete with the healing rest required to begin another week.

As both God and man, Jesus himself napped when needed, sought solitude, and spent time at the temple, all while completing the work his Father assigned. We would do well to follow his example to find solutions for accomplishing our duties while prioritizing worship and relaxation.

Pray Aloud

Lord, you created and modeled rest. Give me wisdom to honor the Sabbath and use the restorative time you initiated. Amen.

Live the Lesson

Evaluate your typical weekends during the school year. Is worship a priority? What saboteurs invade your Sundays? Can adjustments be made to include more rest, recreation, and family time? Set goals before school begins.

Extra Credit

Read Hebrews 4:1–11. Look for truths taught in these verses about a Sabbath rest.

Will I Teach Again?

Read Aloud Philippians 1:6 (ESV)
And I am sure of this, that he who began a good work in you will bring it to completion at the day of Jesus Christ.

A friend posted this question on social media recently: "What if God wants me in the classroom again?" The accompanying picture displayed her many boxes of supplies and books, waiting to be unpacked, stored, or discarded. This friend and I had taught in the same school at one time. Then God led us in separate directions. Since then, we both have relocated again, each time cleaning out classrooms, packing up supplies, and leaving a few items—and a piece of our hearts—behind.

My endings usually accompanied a move due to my husband's work. Like my friend, I have wondered, *will I teach again?* During the COVID outbreak, many left the classroom due to extreme stress and unusual circumstances. Some were ready to retire. How do we know when our time is done? Necessary endings are a part of life. But it can be difficult to discern when to pack the classroom for good.

When Paul penned the words above to his friends in Philippi, he was under house arrest and faced an uncertain future. Yet his situation did not deter him from encouraging those who continued in the faith and in the work to advance Christ's kingdom. Indeed, his letter contained messages of joy and thankfulness as he urged the believers to remain faithful. Despite his confinement, Paul trusted God for his future and for the kingdom work to continue in God's way.

Although our future remains a mystery, we can be certain that God, who works in and through us, will guide our steps and carry out his perfect plan.

Pray Aloud
Lord, only you know my future. Today, this is where you have me. Remove any worry I may have about tomorrow. Give me wisdom each day to trust in you. Amen.

Live the Lesson
Write this week's verse on a 3x5 card. Affix it in an area where you will be reminded often of God's perfect plan for your life and commit it to memory.

Extra Credit
Read Philippians 1. What lessons can we learn from Paul about his attitude toward this life?

Eternal Education

Read Aloud Hebrews 4:12 (ESV)
For the word of God is living and active, sharper than any two-edged sword, piercing to the division of soul and of spirit, of joints and of marrow, and discerning the thoughts and intentions of the heart.

One summer afternoon, a mom sat on her porch sporting her reading glasses and studying her laptop. When her young son approached, he looked at her screen and said, "Sheesh! That's a ton of words. What is that?"

"It's a textbook," she explained. "For the class I'm taking. I have a test this week."

"Oh no!" the boy cried. "Does that mean we go to school for the rest of our lives?!"

Whether working toward an advanced degree or simply meeting professional development requirements, many of us use summer months to squeeze in the classes necessary to continue teaching. With new technology and curriculum changes, our learning never stops.

Similarly, our knowledge and understanding of the Bible continue to develop as long as we live. Each time we read the familiar biblical events or study well-known Bible concepts, God strengthens our faith and gives us a deeper level of understanding. Our Hebrews verse explains this mystery by describing God's Word as "living and active," meaning the Bible is full of life and is working as long as our hearts continue to beat.

Scripture never fails to convict, teach, and mold our thinking when we read and study its contents.

Whether or not our summer months involve learning the latest teaching strategies or gaining expertise, we would be wise to give space and time for daily intake of God's Word. Like our teaching careers, our spiritual growth should be considered eternal education.

Pray Aloud

Jesus, I want to learn more about you and grow in my faith. Speak to me through my daily Bible reading and strengthen my prayer life. Amen.

Live the Lesson

Start a Bible study or Bible reading plan. Develop the habit of reading Scripture every day and continue the routine into the school year.

Extra Credit

Read Psalm 119. God's Word is described in multiple ways throughout this long chapter. Look for the variations and benefits of studying Scripture.

Walking in Tandem

Read Aloud 2 Samuel 22:33–37

It is God who arms me with strength
and keeps my way secure.
He makes my feet like the feet of a deer;
he causes me to stand on the heights.
He trains my hands for battle;
my arms can bend a bow of bronze.
You make your saving help my shield;
your help has made me great.
You provide a broad path for my feet,
so that my ankles do not give way.

A family sat on a flat rock under a towering pine tree. After four miles up and down the mountain path, their feet ached. Relieved of their packs, they chugged water and munched on snacks.

The youngest wiped his dripping brow and asked, "Are we almost to the campsite?"

"Not quite," his mom said. "We'll head over one last mountain, then down again."

"Don't worry about that now," his dad added. "Enjoy the shade. We'll rest before tackling the next trail." The message behind his own words floated back to him. *Take in the scenery. Enjoy this family time. Don't think about faculty meetings next week.*

King David's remarkable ascent to the throne is recorded for us in 2 Samuel, including his early anointing, followed by a boyhood battle with a giant. Those inaugural trials set the pace for the twists and turns David would endure on his upward climb. Throughout the journey, God walked beside David, providing the stamina to progress. David recognized his successes, past and future, depending not on his own abilities, but on God's strength and power.

David's recorded victories remind us of God's continuing work to equip and strengthen his children. He did not fail David. He will not fail us. As we approach a new school year, rest assured we do not travel alone. Our faithful Lord walks in tandem with us through the lows and highs securing our step.

After their break, the family embarked on the next stage of their adventure. Although teacher meetings commenced in one short week, the father took his young son's hand and put the future out of his mind.

Pray Aloud
Heavenly Father, I need your might and power. Provide the energy and skills required to succeed in the coming year. Keep my feet from slipping and my eyes on you. Amen.

Live the Lesson
As you look toward another school year, consider God's track record in your own life. Take note of those occasions when God proved himself faithful.

Extra Credit
Read Psalm 18. List all the metaphors used by David to describe the Lord.

Topical Index

Our Calling as Teachers

Fresh Start 5
Christ in Any Classroom 11
Contentment 19
Unexpected Thanks 27
Fifty-Six More Days 67
Uprooted 91
Will I Teach Again? 107

Our Spiritual, Physical, Mental Health

A Disastrous Day 23
Failure or Favored 31
The Day I Became a Boys' PE Teacher 33
Storytelling 49
Sunday Preparations 53
Fighting Insecurity 61
A Steady Race 77
There's a Snake in Our School! 79
Mary Had a Little Goat 81
Used Up 87
Joy Lost and Found 89
A Time for Everything 97
Sabbath Saboteurs 105
Eternal Education 109

Our Witness

Actions and Words 17
Go and Tell 21
Christmas Wonder 35
Audible Witness 41

Topical Index

"Jesus People" 47
The Power of a Picture 59
Wardrobe Malfunction 71
Show the Glow.................................... 73

Staff and Faculty

Colleagues or Competitors?........................ 15
Each One Is a Gift................................ 45
When We Blow It................................. 55
School Unity 63
The Workers Are Few 69

Strength and Protection, God's

Police Protection or God's Protection? 7
Supernatural Strength 37
The Great Protector............................... 75
"I Can" Statement................................ 93
Independence.................................... 95
Unexpected Storm 103
Walking in Tandem 111

Students and Families

New Roster....................................... 3
Homeless 9
He Knows Every Hair and Every Need............. 13
The Toughest Class Yet 25
Love and Pray 39
Jesus, Help Me................................... 43
Christ's Lunch Lesson 51
Swarming.. 65
A Final Blessing 83
Donut Encounter................................. 99
Summer Surrender 101

Acknowledgments

I am eternally grateful to the Lord Jesus and the Holy Spirit for prompting me to write this devotional. While my eyes sought other projects, you led me past tempting byways and seemingly missed dreams. Once surrendered to you, this work took flight. I commit this project to you.

Thank you John Herring and Iron Stream Media for recognizing the need for this work and taking a chance on me.

To Word Weavers Pensacola and Destin chapters, my invaluable partners of the pen, your encouragement, honesty, and expertise helped hone my skills and made me sound smarter. I appreciate you beyond words.

To my partners in prayer, though you saw little of my work in progress, the efforts on your knees were received in the heavens and were deeply appreciated by this author.

I am deeply grateful to my parents, Richard Walther and Doris Walther-Conrad, as well as my grandparents, Fred and Amanda Walther. Their commitment to Jesus and Lutheran education established a legacy of shaping students' hearts and minds that continues today.

A special thank-you to the many education teams with whom I have been privileged to serve. Although I left a piece of my heart with each departure, I carried away valuable learning, friendships, and precious memories.

Finally, to all teachers who continue to show up, you have my heartfelt appreciation. My prayers continue for you who dedicate your lives to the education of future generations.

About the Author

Gretchen Huesmann's greatest passion is connecting little and big people to Jesus. After earning her bachelor's degree in early childhood education at Concordia University, Chicago, Gretchen taught in private and public settings across seven states. Today, she speaks nationwide to educators, ministry workers, and women's groups. An award-winning author, Gretchen writes for the International School Project website and Hope-Full Living Devotions. She is a member of Word Weavers International and serves as president of her local chapter. You can find her free e-book, *Teachers' Prayer Companion: Prayer Guides for Education Teams*, on her website: gretchenhuesmann.com. Gretchen and her pastor husband have raised four fabulous children and are enjoying their empty nest in northwest Florida.

Photo credit: Malcolm Yawn

Connect with Gretchen